WALTER WANGERIN, JR.

SHAPING OUR LIVES WITH
WORDS OF POWER

**An indepth study of
the writings of Walter Wangerin, Jr.**

by Dianne R. Portfleet

ISBN: 0-9652129-0-4

Library of Congress
Catalog Card Number: 96-094304

Published by Greenleaf - Witcop Press
Distribution, Suite 2
2411 O'Brien SW
Grand Rapids, Michigan 49544
Phone: (616) 791-7052
Fax: (616) 791-7380

Acknowledgments

Grateful acknowledgment is given to the following publishers for permission to
quote from their publications.

AUGSBURG PRESS
Potter

HARPER COLLINS PUBLISHERS
The Book of God
The Book of Sorrows
Elizabeth and the Water Troll
Little Lamb, Who Made Thee?
The Manger is Empty
Measuring the Days
A Miniature Cathedral
Miz Lil and the Chronicles of Grace
Mourning into Dancing
The Orphean Passages
Ragman and Other Cries of Faith
Reliving the Passion
Thistle

THOMAS NELSON PUBLISHERS
As for Me and My House
In the Beginning there was No Sky

SIMON & SCHUSTER BOOKS, NEW YORK
Branta and the Golden Stone
The Crying for a Vision

To Terrance and Matthew
For their support and encouragement

CONTENTS

Shaping our lives with Words of Power

Preface

Things happen in the naming. 'Light!' said God;
At once light straked the nothingness - from no Where,
from the mouth of God. No, it was not
As though bright, fiery horses reared, as though
They plunged mane-flaming through the dark because
God ordered them abroad, lights lighting out
At God's command. The speaking didn't cause
Light. His word was light, primal in his mouth.

Naming things creates them. Look out! I stand
At the black rim of the universe on nothing,
Facing you, about to talk. Not command --
I won't command nor ask nor risk rebuffing.

No, I will merely say the word, and we
Will be, and you will be in love with me."

"But Speak the Word Only"
Walter Wangerin, Jr.

When I first discovered <u>The Book of the Dunn Cow</u> by Walter Wangerin, Jr. in 1979, I was immediately drawn to it for I sensed that here was a writer who truly took the craft and the content of writing seriously, and who knew the power of words and their potential effect upon the reader. His subsequent works have only served to reinforce that original impression. In all of his writings his words are words of power truthfully naming the reality in which we live, creating a cosmos out of the chaos of daily life, and enabling the reader to hear and to see more clearly the meaningful love of God and the harmony behind the more visible discord and restlessness of daily life.

I trust that this brief introduction to Wangerin's work will encourage many to read his writings and to understand the depth and mythological wholeness of his excellent art.

As he truthfully names reality (both visible and invisible), he encourages us to honestly examine our lives so that we will with childlike wonder once again see beyond the limited, one-sided vision of our lives to the significance behind them.

Wangerin talks to us as his readers, and his words "cause to be what had not been before." His words create. And "although only God performs this creative function purely, yet dimly and in a mimic," Wangerin as a poet, "causes to be what had not been before. He sings and there gathers under the heart of his hearer the pressure of his music, the swelling of a new word, like an infant..." And just as this "creating power of language is potent," so Wangerin's writings are powerful, and we "wince with wonder" as his "language stuns us with a name -- and with being."

Dianne R. Portfleet, 1996

Chapter I.

MYTHS, STORIES, AND SEEING LIFE WHOLLY

Shaping our lives with Words of Power

MYTHS, STORIES, AND
SEEING LIFE WHOLLY

"In order to comprehend the experience one is living in, he must, by imagination and by intellect, be lifted out of it. He must be given to see it whole; but since he can never wholly gaze upon his own life while he lives it, he gazes upon the life that in symbol comprehends his own. Art presents such lives, such symbols. Myth especially, persisting as a mother of truth through countless generations -- myth presents, myth is, such a symbol, shorn and unadorned, refined and true.

And when the one who gazes upon that myth suddenly in dreadful recognition, cries out 'There I am. That is me!' then the marvelous translation has occurred: he is lifted out of himself to see himself wholly."

Stories and myths - two key elements of Walter Wangerin, Jr.'s artistic endeavors - true stories and myths of ultimate truth which our culture with its scientific, rational mode of thought has so ignored yet now so desperately needs - these form the essence of this truthful, often "terrifyingly" honest writer.

Behind his art, his use of myth, and his intense storytelling is Wangerin's dominating conviction that the storyteller is crucial to the healthy survival of a community. "A community of people may exist without art and literature - not well, and they may be crippled, but they can exist...But a culture that explodes its myths and no longer tells stories becomes chaotic -- the cosmos no longer makes sense. Community is broken, covenant is broken, and cosmos is lost." (lecture at Calvin, April, 1995)

Wangerin defines the storyteller using an old term, Scop, the shaper of life, and an even older definition of poet, "A piler into piles and a heaper into heaps." And he sees the role of the storyteller (poet) as being that of bringing cosmos out of the chaos of our lives, and providing us with symbols, or objective correlatives, which enable the reader to see the patterns running through life. "The storyteller is the one who traces the patterns running through other people's lives and expresses them through a choice of words, who interprets by his choice of details and words, the reality that has been there all along, unseen. The storyteller is the visionary who can bring into focus the blurred image, the artist who can set down not only what is apparent, but what can be perceived behind the visible." (Berger, p. 31)

Wangerin's powerful prose enables us to catch a glimpse of ourselves and of the glory of God behind everyday mundane life, and, as a result, his writings are invaluable to the reader searching for the truth and for the Christian community attempting both to understand itself and God's often silent workings in its midst.

Wangerin explained in his article "Telling Tales" that his stories "are moments of intensest interaction, when God's presence for good or evil, is felt so strongly that every other thing, every detail or gesture, is defined by that presence. These moments, strung together, form the history of religion. They are both remembered and retold as stories, for they were, at first, events. They are significant; they testify each time they are told to a timeless relationship with the Deity."

"But they are also signifying: that is, they make sense of the experiences which people suffer in the present, the common stuff of their lives...In this way people are relieved of confusion - not as though their lives were explained to them intellectually and they understood, but rather as though a loving and powerful parent came and put arms around them, and they were comforted." (Wangerin, "Telling Tales")

Although Wangerin draws the stories from his own family and life experiences, he many times adds or deletes details to better emphasize a truth, for he is not attempting to accurately portray actual events; and even though his stories, thus, are not necessarily factual, they are truth. And "The aim of fiction is absolute and honest truth. Truth, mind you, not facts." (Chekhov, quoted from L'Engle, The Rock that is Higher, p. 105)

4

Wangerin's stories are "true, not necessarily accurate -- they picture behind the material realities to the workings of God - ultimate truth." "My stories do not instruct in definitional, doctrinal meanings...My stories by their very ambiguity do better than that: My stories make a cosmos out of chaos, and therefore, they comfort. Whereas doctrines define, find balances, classify, and report, stories cause wholeness. Doctrines may engage the understanding mind, but story engages the human whole -- so the human who was fragmented is put together again through the hearing of his/her story."

Wangerin in his work, The Crying for a Vision, describes the true stories told by the Lacota Indians: "In this culture *wayakape* or *wicowayake* are "true stories, in which the teller's license to alter event and character in recounting a historical incident is assumed. The meaning and effect of the story which need only be based on fact take precedence over a record-keeping sense of history." In the same way Wangerin intuitively selects significant memories (he does not just record a factual history), purifies the details, sweats away the irrelevance to tell a story that is good, as well as true. As Black Elk, a Lacota storyteller, recounts: "Stories are oral rainbows in which the totality of experience appears temporarily to our consciousness before it fades. It always comes after conflict, and it remains just long enough in our view to remind us all is well and that it will return but only after more threatening conflict." (Julian Rice, Lacota Storytelling, p. 38)

Wangerin in his role as truthful storyteller, has to describe a human being honestly by describing his imperfections, his sins, his sorrows, as well as his triumphs. Thus, as Wangerin states, "Many who read my writing today are inclined to call me 'melancholy.' They are wrong. Anderson's fantasies schooled me, rather, in realism. And as a writer, I know no resurrection except that first there's been a death. And as a writer, I cannot speak genuinely or deeply of resurrection except I speak of death and the sin that engendered death. That I speak accurately of death without despairing is hardly 'melancholic.'" (Wangerin, "Reality and the Vision") In order to truthfully show forth cosmos out of the chaos of our world, the cosmos must be powerfully and accurately described. Wangerin's fictional world is not one that is organized in settled formulae and principles. It is not the prose world of moral instruction, problem solving, or clarification. It is a poetic world shaped by the news of the Gospel of Christ and shaped in fictional language which takes the risk that the reader or hearer will read or hear it as fantasy or falsehood. But his fiction is an alternative mode of speech to render God's truth; speech that is dramatic, artistic, and invitatory, and pushes out the edges of our mundane, chaotic world in which most of us are trapped. (Bruggemann, p. 8)

Wangerin constantly experiments with form, different genres and diverse voices to render reality truthfully and to show forth the ultimate truth behind the everyday events. One technique that Wangerin employees so well in his works is that of the objective correlative -- that symbol or character that enables the reader to experience the exact emotion and to experience what the author is attempting to convey in his work. Thus, Wangerin's characters become the symbols for our own lives, so that we can objectively look at ourselves, suffer the emotions of the character, and be changed by the experience. For example, after Orpheus undergoes much change in his drama with God, the narrator of The Orphean Passages announces to the reader that the experience of death and resurrection has become our experience personally as a reader, truly, and he is "writing that our joy may be complete." He is indeed.

Each of Wangerin's works evokes from the reader responses to the ultimate truths of the universe -- sin, death, forgiveness, resurrection. And these are the truths that form the basis of his stories and his retelling of myths from older and different cultures. These truths are seen in his first book, The Book of the Dunn Cow, and its sequel, The Book of Sorrow, as his personified animals not only reflect but illustrate the mythical truths underlying the world - sin, pride, humans as guardians against evil, death, love, forgiveness, and resurrection.

"Many thousands of creatures lived on this still unwary earth. These were the animals, whom God notices in his passage above. And the glory of it was that they were there for a purpose. To be sure, very few of them recognized the full importance of their being and of their being there; and that ignorance endangered terribly the good fulfillment of their purpose. But God so let it be; and did not choose to force knowledge upon the animals.

What purpose? Simply, the animals were the Keepers, the Watchers, the Guards. They were the last protection against an almighty evil, which should it pass them, would burst bloody into the universe and smash into chaos and sorrow everything that had been made both orderly and good."

Thus Wangerin begins his two novels of these animals, these keepers of the evil, and his story shows forth to the reader the conflicts, struggles with evil, and the potential for chaos and disorder in the world. Wangerin refuses to moralize in his stories, refuses to be dogmatic and explain his words, and many times because of these refusals his stories undefine and become "lightning bolts in the midst of a herd of cattle." The stories become dangerous and ambiguous because he allows the individual reader to hear and to interpret the stories, and he allows for ambiguities in interpretations. His stories do not explicitly say what they mean, but they themselves are the meaning and stand for themselves. Much like Henry James, Wangerin's stories "render but don't report. They show but do not tell. Thus the verbs are active not passive...and the storyteller doesn't talk about the story, but shows it." And after he finishes his novel or fictional work, it has to bear the responsibility of its own meaning...It is now a thing apart from the writer. It is nearer now to the reader. Thus, in Wangerin's fictional works, the reader is led into the faither's journey with God through many passages of the drama. And even his children's books (or especially his children's books) become fairy tales tracing the ultimate truths of sin, death and resurrection. In all of these, Wangerin invites "his reader to see how God's strange grace operates in action and character. And through the clearness and the simplicity of the stories, the readers are drawn through them to God." (Andraski, p. 30-33)

"The work becomes its own cosmos for a little while, and the reader is invited to enter into this world. After entering into this work, the reader brings the experiences of it into the real world, and the work may become the 'lens' through which the viewer makes sense of the rest of existence. This is what stories have done from the beginning."

Wangerin truly believes that there is power in words to change the soul of a person, and although this power is invisible in story and art, it is there. The writer who can use words with power can influence and change people through his/her words. This power is two-edged for it can bring order and cosmos out of randomness, or it can destroy others and tell lies and change people to believe lies. As a result, he sharply distinguishes between "good" art and "bad" art. Like T. S. Eliot, he believes that the "greatness of literature cannot solely be determined by literary standards." A literary work can be excellent judged by literary standards and still be considered "bad" art. "The fiction that we read affects our behavior toward our fellow humans, affects our patterns of ourselves. We read of humans behaving in certain ways, with the approval of the author, who gives his benediction to this behavior by his attitude the result of the behavior arranged by himself, and we can be influenced towards behaving in the same way...The author of a work of imagination is trying to affect us wholly, as human beings, whether he knows it or not, and we are affected by it, as human beings, whether we intend to be or not." For Wangerin, "bad" literature leaves the reader in chaos, with despair, or portrays "seen" reality only, totally omitting the ultimate truth behind this visible reality. Or it may present "hope" with no serious confrontation with evil or death, and thus cripples us in our fight against and recognition of evil both in our world and in our lives. "The stories that don't tell .of evil cripple us...Evil must be named and woven into the stories so that the good can also be woven in. One-sided stories cripple us. (Wangerin, Anderson) But style, artistic skill, serious thought, and ultimate truth concerning good and evil must all be a part of "good art." As he states in "A Review of Today's Good Writing and Good Writers": "A devout person is not necessarily a good writer. Books faithful to certain principles of doctrine may be wretchedly faithless to principles of good literature...No matter how true the truth, it is affected by the form in which it is presented. Cheap language will make the message seem cheap...Shoddy prose presents a slipshod truth...but just because an author writes with consummate skill, with vigor and power and beauty doesn't mean the writer also writes the truth. A good writer is not necessarily a writer of goodness, nor is good writing necessarily worthy of my good faith and trust...Words must finally mean something...Effective art is a subtle, pervasive persuader. It teaches the people how to 'see' by giving them sight and insight in an intense, controlled experience....There are two standards, then, by which to judge the value of literature of this day: its form and its meaning....Does it (however realistic its vision, however true to the wounds of humanity) elevate?"

Another contemporary author, Chiam Potok, further explains these ideas of the power of art and language in his work, The Gift of Asher Lev. Asher Lev, a young artist, paints good pictures and hurts the people he loves. The Rebbe explains art to Asher as he

8

confides in him: "My father once said that the seeing of God is not like the seeing of man. Man sees between the blinks of his eyes. He does not know what the world is like during the blinks. He sees the world in pieces, fragmented. But the Master of the Universe sees the world whole, unbroken. That world is good. Our seeing is broken, Asher Lev. Can we make it like the seeing of God?...An artist must see the world whole; he must somehow learn to see during the blinks; he must see the connections, the betweenness in the world. Even if the connections are ugly and evil, the artist must learn to see and record them...And then if an artist truly sees...then he will see that all is good."

Wangerin in his fictional works records all that he has learned to see, even the evil and the ugly, and he uses all of his artistic creativity and skill to portray this reality, but then he sees behind the blinks to the workings of God, and then uses his powerful language to portray the hope and goodness even in the midst of ugliness and death.

Wangerin, through his realism, the prism of his fiction through which we see evil, suffering, and death, enables us both to understand the chaos and bewilderment and sorrow of our individual and collective lives, and to see the cosmos behind them. "An artist of faith - a real artist - will therefore cry: Listen we have a myth that consoles and secures, one worthy of a lasting belief, one we can surely live by. It is 'myth' insofar as it is the timeless, defining story by which we make sense of a senseless existence. But it is truth insofar as it happened. It is vaster than I am (says the author). I did not create it; it created me. I may name it with my words, but it is the word which names me first: Jesus Christ." ("What's a Good Story?") So we can see in The Book of Sorrows, even amidst the deaths and deep sufferings and hurts, the word of hope at the end as the evil within Chauntecleer is recognized and released: "As Chauntecleer dies in the middle of his laugh...Pertelote lifted up her voice and began to sing on the battlefield. She sang as though she walked the rim of the universe, like the moon, a pale and lovely presence here on earth."

"While she sang, the grey Wolf Chinook left the form of Boreas and came to Pertelote and bowed her head and listened....While she sang, the Animals lifted their heads from sleep and looked at the sky and saw the stars...and they resolved never to forget the song or the singer...And far, far away the Brothers mice pulled their noses from the circle in which they slept. 'Listen,' they said. 'Do you hear that? The dear Lady Pertelote is singing Compline.'

"And Chalcedony the crippled Hen touched the Fawn to waken her, 'Listen, listen, child,' she said. 'Tis seldom in a lifetime you shall hear an angel sing.'"

After so much sorrow, evil has been recognized, and chaos has been defeated and there is unity, cosmos, and singing in the world. In the same way in <u>The Crying for a Vision</u>, the circle of life which had been broken through so much pride and sorrow and the myths and dances which had ceased are restored through the death of Moves Walking: "By daylight the buffaloes were wearing the common brown colors, and we were glad. Tantanka was back. Our brother was home. The famine was over and we could hunt again. Oh, there was so much work to be done. But first we had to give thanks: Pila miya Tunkashila! We danced in a sacred circle and we sang new songs and we cried in sorrow and we laughed in happiness because Wakan Tanka had decided to send us the red and blue days again." And in <u>The Orphean Passages</u>, Orpheus dies to self, loses all that he has, but his mourning is turned to dancing, for "he sees the Lord, and he crosses from Black Saturday to Resurrection Sunday. Then he can pray in perfect peace, straight into the ear of Jesus."

Although these works all end in hope after much sorrow, Wangerin never sacrifices his excellent writing or his religious faith by using "cheap" language, bringing in an artificial ending, or by not mastering the techniques of the language. And his writing always adheres to both good "form and substance" - good "sound and sense." As he states, "Art must always obey the best technical conventions of its craft, and it must be truth. It must love beauty, and it must love truth. The truth of the finest art, though it decry the sin in us with accurate depictions, must also cry us upward...and do it with craft as crafty as the Creator's!" And Wangerin uses language effectively, artistically, and has mastered the craft of his trade.

Any attempt to explain how Wangerin accomplishes the task of making visible the invisible workings of God in this world involves a look at his use of mythology. Wangerin believes that even "pagan" myths or myths from diverse cultures, if they reflect the universe truly, can be used to help us understand God, Christ, and our drama with Him. As he states in <u>The Orphean Passages</u>: "Can Divine truth be discovered by this intermediary of a pagan myth? I think so, truly; the myth is not one storyteller's creation; it has the sanction and the commonality of all peoples; it spoke to yearnings universally suffered; it hinted answers universally satisfying; it crept very close to the universality of God himself. The vital distinction between its word and the word of God, then, is certainly not that myth lies, but rather that it merely images what God performs. It remains forever a story, but God makes history. It asks; God answers. It symbols; but God is. It is true, but God is Truth."

With this understanding of myth as symbolizing what God does, Wangerin weaves mythological stories throughout his fiction, uses them to illustrate the workings of God in our world which our rational, factual language limits, and creates with it a cosmos where ultimate truth and kairos (God's time) lift us out of our mundane lives so that we can see them wholly.

Thus, in his work <u>The Crying for a Vision</u> Wangerin uses the myths of the Lacota to help us understand not only this culture but our own lives. "In them (the Lacotas), therefore, may any people see itself....In their spirit, their stories, their legends may an 'other-people' find itself reflected...This people has named and known itself. A shining self-awareness. A public give away. For in them knowledge becomes a song, and songs are sung and anyone can listen and someone might learn....For my story presents the Lacota as *ovate icke* indeed, that common people in whom all peoples might see themselves. Therefore, good and evil mix in them just as virtue and vice exist together in any one family or nation on earth. For I have found in the Lacota vision a rich analogue for the relationship any people of genuine faith experiences with creation and the Creator. It was my fortune, then -- and my artistic choice -- to use their world as the controlling metaphor of this novel."

> "Reader, *wachin ksapa yo*! Look not at the
> tale but through it for the truth."

Wangerin's world is filled with such metaphors and myths to enable the reader to transcend the mundane world long enough to get a glimpse of its wholeness, so that that vision will become a lens through which he "truthfully" views the daily events of life. Wangerin intertwines various myths and legends throughout his works, "sometimes whole, sometimes just the threads, taking the tone and the vision of the legend but making the narrative new." Even his children's stories are woven throughout with myths creating beautiful fairy tales that enable the child (and adult) reader to clearly see the ultimate truths of the Christian faith: sin, death, resurrection, love, forgiveness, sacrifice, death of false pride. In Potter, the story of a young boy who encounters the death of his friend and his own serious illness, the legend of the Phoenix is used to make knowable and felt the truth of the resurrection. "'Five hundred years' sang the Oriole, a misty song: 'Once every half one thousand years, the story of God takes place for us, and the birds are reminded, and the birds remember. The birds know the love of God. Hurry Potter, that you might see the story. Hurry, my brother, that you might know it, too.'" As the story progresses, and Potter sees and loves the beautiful Phoenix, it dies, and Potter is heartbroken. "The Oriole said, 'I brought you to see the story, Potter, and here you are, and isn't it strange that I have to tell it to you after all...' On the third day the Oriole scolded him: 'Pish, Potter, here is a blockhead for you! The very thing I brought you here to see is now before you. The wonder of God is on two legs and his mercy is here in the flesh, and the birds who miss it count themselves unlucky, and that is the most of the birds -- but you! You feel sorry for yourself and so you mock the gift of God...Potter, Potter, the Phoenix is alive again! Potter! The dead, they do not die forever. Nay, they rise again! Birds by the Phoenix, children by the love of God...Look, Potter. Let the blockhead see and believe.'

"Potter gazed at the Phoenix...He began to giggle. He whooped, and he plain laughed...He let go his branch and went after the Phoenix...a great cloud of witnesses, thousands of birds -- they flew with the joy of life, life not overcome by death...and all their song was Hallelujah!'"

Wangerin uses these metaphors, myths, and symbols to enable the reader to go past the clichés of his/her religion and to hear again and to see again the tremendous truth of God which gets forgotten or lost so quickly in everyday life. As Walter Brueggeman states: "The gospel is too readily heard and taken for granted, as though it contained no unsettling news...The gospel of Christ is thus a truth widely held, but a truth greatly reduced. It is truth that has been flattened, trivialized, and rendered inane. Our technical way of thinking reduces mystery to problem, transforms assurance into certitude...and so takes the categories of Biblical faith and represents them into manageable shapes. We need an alternative mode of speech to preach the good news: speech that is dramatic, artistic, capable of inviting people in...unembarrassed by concreteness. Such speech would assault our imagination and push out the presumed world in which most of us are trapped." ("Finally Comes the Poet")

Wangerin in his fiction, and in his other writings, uses this daring, imaginative, poetic speech to break us out of our one-sided vision and to enable us to see beyond the visible world. He doesn't offer moral instruction or doctrinal clarification or problem solving in his works; he offers us the possibility of a "new existence shaped by the news of the Gospel." By doing this type of writing, Wangerin always runs the risk of being misunderstood or being heard only as a fantasy writer or as a writer of falsehoods. But the important point to be emphasized is that for Wangerin the story of Christ is the true story, the only story that Christians have to tell and that it has no unstoried form. His fictions drive us beyond the "known, accurate" truths of our culture to the ultimate truth, and they sometimes seem so incredible as to strain the imagination -- but God's truth is so incredible as to be hard to believe, and his stories accurately reflect this truth that "the fictions of God are truer than the facts of men." (I Cor. 1:25)

These concepts of the story of Christ being told in poetic language are well seen in <u>Branta and the Golden Stone</u>. Branta's father has been one of the Magi, and he keeps the golden stone which the Christ child had touched, and this was the "power of the stone that it changed people. It made them whatever they wanted to be. It made sick people healthy, it gave sight to the blind, and it caused the crippled to walk....But do you know the danger of the stone?...Whatever the people became they had to stay that way forever." After her father's death, Branta learns the meaning of love, and the length of sacrifice and what Christ's incarnation meant to him and to us, and the person who hears or reads the story is enabled to feel with the heart ideas that were only in the head before. Wangerin's poetic and metaphorical language enables the reader to overcome the dissociation of sensibility that has occurred many times in our lives, so that once again we understand and feel the riches, potentialities, and dangers of our faith as well as its sacrifices and joys. His stories are not new truths but rather ones that we have long known yet have allowed to be greatly reduced.

Even when Wangerin tells the story of Christ to children in his book <u>The Baby Jesus</u>, he tells it in the form of a fairy tale because the Bible is a story book of marvelous true stories sharing the moments of God's interactions in the world. As he states in the preface: "Most of the sweet, victorious tales in this world are fairy tales. In them the child is allowed to imagine evil overcome.

"But there is one tale which is no one's imagination, which is true and therefore very powerful: the story of Jesus. Here we do not say to the child, 'Imagine' but we say 'Believe.' We do not pretend that a little girl had a fairy godmother to help her. Rather we announce in fact that a real child had a real God to help and to love her...The story of Jesus. It is a beautiful tale, a terrible tale, and then again a tale more beautiful than any other. For, that God should come to love is beautiful. That he should fight the devil, suffer the hatred of a sinful world, and die -- these things are too true (as children know) and terrible. But wait! That he should rise to life again, triumphant over evil, and that he should wish to share the triumph with his children is the most beautiful news of all."

Wangerin, in all of his works, takes the general, eternal truth of God's revelation, and combines it with the particular culture and daily events of his characters so that the distance between the readers and the stories of God is decreased - a distance of time or culture that often makes the Scriptural stories seem strange and disconnected from or irrelevant to our individual lives. These particular events are then seen as part of a continuous whole and purpose. The isolated episodes of his stories begin to make sense as Wangerin intertwines them together with the eternal stories of God. His stories are not for simple entertainment (though they are extremely entertaining), they are like spiritual medicines which can provide transformation.

These experiences of his and his watchful approach to the lives of others form a vital part of his art through which he "communicates truth with the impact of personal experiences." And this impact on the reader is "subtle but pervasive, and it teaches people how to 'see' by giving them a particular perspective, sight and insight, in an intense, controlled experience....Art shapes the reader's view of truth."

Chapter II.

CHARACTERS - THE HEART OF WANGERIN'S WRITINGS

Shaping our lives with Words of Power

CHARACTERS - THE HEART
OF WANGERIN'S WRITINGS

"The contemporary Orpheus is an example of one moving through the passages of faithing, but he is not exemplary. He is drawn fully human, as anyone experiencing the full length of a relationship with God must be fully human: faulty, sinning some sins consciously and others unconsciously, sometimes very clear about his own condition, sometimes fearfully obtuse, yet able, withal to love sincerely and to believe in the Lord God on many levels.

Surely, I do not enjoin the reader to be like him. Nor ought anyone to seek in him an ideal. Rather, I say as this Orpheus does, so do we enact our drama with God. And even as we are, every one of us, complicated individuals of ingenious slights and devisings, baffling even to ourselves, so is he. He is not always to be trusted; but his story is."

Wangerin creates memorable characters in his works who develop, grow, err, yet become mirrors for the reader through whom the reader can see himself wholly and can be lifted out of himself to understand his drama with God a little more clearly. Although all of his characters are minutely described and locked in time and location, their stories are universal truths which all readers recognize. And the detailed physical descriptions give us a sense of cosmos and safety so that we dare enter into the world of these characters and experience their stories and, like the child Wangerin when his father read him stories of Hans Christian Andersen, so when we read the "final sentences of his stories we

17

are crying, we are laughing, we are tingling. For we are not learning, but rather are experiencing the highest truths of our faith...We discover these truths in experience, not in remote and intellectual lessons that our poor brains can scarcely translate into 'real life.'" ("Telling Tales")

Wangerin's characters are the objective correlatives through whom Wangerin translates the truths of Christianity into "real life." And because they are not typical "heroes" who are too perfect to be identified with, we can enter their stories, seeing ourselves reflected in them as in a mirror and we can trust the truths of their stories for Wangerin, as an author, has made a serious covenant with the reader to never tell "lies" with his powerful words, but to always tell truth -- truth regarding the reality of our lives and truths regarding the vision of Christianity -- and as one reads his works, one realizes that he is honest in his attempts at truthfulness. And we are shaped by his stories, enabled to see God working in the minute dailyness of life, and signified by his words. And his truth is not one-sided only, for "The truth of the finest art," according to Wangerin, "though it decry the sin in us with accurate depictions, must also cry us upward, call us into relationship with God, revise the 'reality' we had believed in. -- What's a 'good story?' Why it must be a holy thing after all!" ("A Review of Today's Good Literature and Good Writers") The characters he composes and the true-life stories he tells are always developing toward an ideal, and although the ideal may be far off because of the darkness, sorrow and self-centeredness of his character, it is always there shaping the events, leading us, as readers, toward the ideals of the faith. What are those ideals toward which his characters are moving? Honesty, self-knowledge, awareness of their need for God, awareness of their sinfulness, repentance, selfless love, self-sacrifice, total openness to God, hope in the midst of sorrow, rebirth of a new self created by God and controlled by God -- the experience of faithing rather than the head knowledge of it. And since God "leads the faither further unto himself not in a manner divorced from daily and worldly experiences and by the means of the stuff and tumble of life," it is the character, their actions, and the actions of others upon them that become important to Wangerin. Each character goes through a series of epiphanies (some small, some overwhelming) or a series of little deaths -- all of which enable the character to be "killed by God and resurrected in Him." And since all the elements of a person's life combine to make our being, so Wangerin focuses on very minor, sometimes seemingly irrelevant events and happenings to develop his characters.

Wangerin, like William James stated many years ago, believes that "feeling is a deeper source of religion, and that philosophy and theological formulations are secondary products, like translations of a test into another tongue." And today we need to "rediscover our completeness in Christ in stories sacred and profane...It is story and all related art forms that touch us at our deepest levels and convince us of truth...The writer convinces us of the truth by dealing with us wholistically...Writers try to make us feel the truth. Good art gets the truth inside us on a level deeper than the surface of our minds. On this level, truth is most irresistible. The mind may not only resist the truth but may even accept it and keep it at a personal distance. Logical convictions are not necessarily existential aspirations. The writer makes us nostalgic for the beauty we have missed, the life we have forfeited, the meaning which somehow has eluded our grasp. Art haunts us with the spectre of a lost humanity and bids us return to Paradise." (Bausch, Storytelling, p. 11)

Wangerin's characters perform the function of art for they evoke responses from the readers, and because they are so intensely portrayed, Wangerin personally involves the reader in his stories -- there is no personal distance kept, and his stories touch us on a level deeper than the surface of our mind. And his characters are also symbols of a life which comprehends our own, and as we gaze upon his character symbols, "We cry out in dreadful recognition, 'There I am.'" And Wangerin, because he is honestly attempting to portray truth, presents in his characters all of our experiences of life, the griefs, the sins, the deaths, as well as the joys; for as all of his work show, it is "the experience of genuine grief that prepares for joy," and we, who so hide from the truth about ourselves and who so avoid grief, are forced to experience grief and sorrow in Wangerin's characters so that this joy can also be experienced by us. David Neff claims that Wangerin's "iris admits only shadows," and that his art "provides ample insight into his melancholia although they may provide fewer insights into life and the universe where (I suspect) the archangels sing more Glorias than laments)." (David Neff) But Neff misinterprets the realism and sadness of Wangerin's characters for even in the midst of suffering and grief, hope, joy and healing are always present and, as Orpheus learns, "And God loves you. He didn't never not love you. No, but he been waitin' for you, been waitin' ever' day of your life to call you his chil'." And wherever the journey to Easter and Resurrection begins, it must always begin right here at "the contemplation of my death." And Wangerin's stories always "cry us upward, and call us into relationship with God."

Wangerin's characters are there to remind us to "remember." And his works are "mirrors that hide nothing and that hurt us. They reveal an ugliness we would rather deny...And we avoid these mirrors of veracity." But Wangerin, as a truthful artist, refuses to whitewash the truth or to let us see only one side of ourselves; he forces us to courageously look at the mirror, to clearly know ourselves - even our evil - until we admit our need for healing. And this hurt of truly seeing ourselves is purging and precious, and his characters become "mirrors of dangerous grace." And the closer the truths of Christ get to us as the readers of his works, the less we like it because "we feel threatened by the truth." However, the emotional intensity of many of the interactions of his characters as they reveal us to ourselves with all honesty and bareness, always are there to prepare us for significance, hope, love, forgiveness, and joy. Wangerin's works make us uncomfortable, upset our equilibrium, confront us with death for only one reason, so that we can move on to joy and resurrection. These movements can easily be seen from his characters:

Thistle, through her suffering and her belief that Pudge has eaten all the height, strength and beauty in the world, is prepared through this grief for the dancing, laughter, and love at the end; Elizabeth, through the death of the water troll, can laugh and love again; Orpheus, through his darkness, tears, and self-knowledge, "sees the Lord...and can pray in perfect peace;" Fire Thunder can love a small child again and the Lacotas could dance in their sacred circle and give thanks and sing new songs. Whether Wangerin's stories and characters are from Scriptures, his imagination, or real life, each learns through grief and painful self-knowledge to die to self and all that hinders joy, and even to die to temporary happiness so that everlasting joy can be born. As he states in <u>Reliving the Passion</u>: "The difference between shallow happiness and a deep, sustaining joy is sorrow. Happiness lives where sorrow is not. When sorrow arrives, happiness dies. It can't stand pain. Joy, on the other hand, rises from sorrow, and, therefore, can withstand all grief. Joy, by the grace of God, is the transfiguration of suffering into endurance, of endurance into character, and of character into hope -- and the hope that has become our joy does not (as happiness must for those who depend upon it) disappoint us...There can be no resurrection from the dead except first there is death...And Christ's rising is our joy. And then the certain hope of our own resurrection warrants the joy both now and forever."

His characters drawn from the Bible travel the same faithing journey as we do, so throughout his works he retells the stories of the Biblical characters, just as his father's sermons were dramatic, and he would bring to life the characters: Peter denying Christ, John leading the Mother of Jesus away, and these stories translate us to the time of Christ. So Mary Magdelene in The Orphean Passages becomes the contemporary figure who also has gone through our sorrows, and now tells us of the glory: "Sweet, sorrowful and laughing Mary Magdelene, talk to me. Tell me: What was it like to rise again, and to be?...Lady, I know the sorrow that preceded it, how it made mute fools of us; you and I, we cried so hard that our tears blinded us to the abiding truth. We went wailing questions: Where is he? Where is he? Morbid questions...Woman, I know the sorrow. Oh, tell me of the joy...Won't you tell me of the raw thing itself, of the thing made primal and eternal, of life? Won't you tell me how it felt to say, 'I have seen the Lord!'"

Through Wangerin's characters, his collapsing of time so that the events of our lives and the events of 2000 years ago become contemporaneous, he attempts to enable us to be eyewitnesses of the truths of our faith, not secondary hearers, but primary experiencers so that we "experience the truths here and now...and we do not follow cleverly devised myths but are eyewitnesses of his majesty and love," and we walk in the truth both in thought and in genuine feelings. Our disassociation of sensibilities is healed as our intellects and hearts merge, and we -- we are relieved of confusion.

Part of the power of Wangerin's works is that he yearns deeply to experience and to have the reader truly experience the truths of the faith. As he states in the 5th passage of The Orphean Passages: "It is at this point that the experience which Paul declares becomes our experience -- 'experience and no longer the inscrutable catechetic of our youth, experience, our own Way, our vital Truth...our very life.'" And as Wangerin believes, "Great art always persuades us to experience the thing it presents." So he knows that when his art works, the readers experience the deep truths that his characters epitomize.

Wangerin longs for a "bright, convincing, palpable appearing of angels before me - the experience itself in time and space and particularity, as warm as real flame, the memory forever. It is perhaps the child in me; and perhaps it's a confession of weaker faith to beg to see the connectors; but I wish I could. I want to meet the messengers of God, the burning ministers of power and goodness.

> But I never have.
> Almost I can hear the whirr of their wings...
> Almost. Not quite.
> No, not ever.
> And I am sorry for the lack of it."

(Bright Annunciation of Angels)

But in his fiction, and sometimes in the most humble of his characters, Wangerin and we experience the angels of God; we get a glimpse of significance behind the mundane, and we hear the whirr of angel wings. So in the story "Baglady," Wangerin states: "I thought I would tell them of my experience with Robert...It would serve as a kind of warning, in which I was the bad example: 'If we grow cumbered about much serving, we might lose a willing humility and lose a world of good besides...See how near God is to you? Angels do sometimes come in the form of the most oppressed; God is here...'" Then as he later learns in the telling of the story: "Angels, yes indeed! But when angels descend from Cabrini Green and not from condominiums, they don't bathe first; they don't approve themselves with pieties first; they do not fit the figments of Christian imagination; they prophesy precisely as they are and expect us to hear them whole, prophecies and blasphemies together." And all of Wangerin's stories are these moments of intensest encounter when God's presence is felt so strongly that every thing, every detail or gesture, is defined by that presence...And his sharply detailed characters are the messengers through whom we experience God's presence or, as Wangerin says, through whom "God bushwacks us."

In another story as he watches as a young woman dies, he states as he watches the family members minister to her: "I

22

gasped. These were the angels! These were the ministers of the Lord, one accounting for an earthly need, the other for a heavenly one, moved unknowing by the presence of the Almighty, sitting side to side of a tomb going empty before them. I leaned far, far forward, not to miss a thing that the Lord was doing, not a word of his love in Irene's mouth, and this is the time when I wept, but for gladness. God was not absent. He was here in these two. And I saw them fleshy at the loss, soft in the sorrow; but through them I saw the descent and ascent of the messengers of God and heard angelic motion toward a resurrection.

> 'Greater things than these will you see...'
> I saw the love of God at work: Rabboni!
> I have seen the Lord!"

Wangerin realizes as he writes his works and listens to his own life that "there is a divinity that shapes its (the work of art's) way. Events...and people affect the artist. Unplanned experiences leave traces. And though none of these may be identifiable in the final piece, they are there. They are the angels whom God sent to the Mother artist to whisper to her the name of the child she was bearing."

And as his works are read, the reader begins to sense the presence of God's angels in his/her own life as he/she learns to recognize God's messengers in events that would have otherwise gone unnoticed. Not only does Wangerin listen and remember the angels he has seen in his life, but he evokes a similar response in the reader, and the invisible world becomes more visible to us because of his stories.

How does Wangerin accomplish this artistic encounter between the reader and his writing? He tells the myths and Holy histories and stories of Scriptures in conjunction with the present, lesser and more personal stories of the people of the present religious community. As Wangerin explains: "My particular story about Marie stands under my general story with God; each enlightens the other, and I am moved, as it were, a chapter forward in both. But both become one in the telling...my stories do not instruct in definitional, doctrinal meanings. But by their very ambiguity (their plastic ability to admit each individual together with his and her personal variances) they do better than that: they make a cosmos of chaos...Whereas doctrine defines, finds boundaries, classifies and separates, the stories cause wholeness. Doctrines may engage the understanding mind, but story engages the human whole

- body, sense, reason, emotion, memory, laughter, tears -- so the person who is fragmented is put back together again and that under the governance of a new experience -- the hearing of his/her own story told...This sort of wholeness is not a truth to be learned and preserved; it is itself experience, an event which when God is behind to participate in it, becomes the Truth that preserves us."

Once a reader has met Wangerin's characters, seen in them objective correlatives that enable him to see himself more clearly and less fragmented, and has experienced the truth of the stories, this experience is never lost, for through these events one's faith is made more concrete and the reader remembers the "truth" of the doctrines in life. Who can think of compassion and Christian service without thinking of Arthur Forte; who can seek the approval of others without Miz Lil coming to mind; who can go through a child's confirmation and teen years without Wangerin's own children, Mary, Joseph, Talitha and Matthew and their experiences coloring the perceptions; who can see creation without the Lacota and their sacred circles and dances being forefront? Sorrows, mourning, death are all experiences through which the reader can now see the workings of God because in these characters their encounters with God were shown forth, and many of these moments which Wangerin notices and portrays to the readers are events which the reader probably would never have noticed if Wangerin's artistic sensitivity had not isolated them and connected them to eternal truths and made them symbols and images.

His characters are like Charles Dickens' characters, carefully drawn, with their characteristic gestures, which make them uniquely memorable, all brought to the forefront. Thus he describes these peculiar traits (sometimes exaggerating them for effect) in detail: For example in the story "Miz Lil" he writes: "Both Miz Lillian and Douglas -- and she was as short as he was, though neater, thriftier, quiet, and maternal - were fixtures of the inner city neighborhood, as standard as pepper shakers on the table. They made the mean streets neighborly....Miz Lil...hadn't a compulsion to talk. She watched and kept her own counsel, and her words were weightier, therefore....these were the flesh of the inner city..." And when Douglas dies, Wangerin states: "Douglas died while watching 'The Lawrence Welk Show' and eating a piece of pie. Miz Lil was dozing on the sofa at the time." Or as he portrays the man in "Butter, bring Butter!": "I was appalled.

Urine made a salty stench; roaches rained off the walls. The man, sockless and with shoes untied, had crumbs on two day's growth of whiskers. There were potato chips in his hand." Or as he describes Odessa Williams: "I had learned, for my own protection, to check her mouth as soon as I entered her room. If the woman wore dentures, she was mad: she wanted her words to click with clarity, to snap and hiss with a precision to her anger. Mad at me, she needed teeth. But if she smiled a toothless smile on me, then I knew that her language would be soft and I had her approval -- that week....One little lamp shed an orange light on the hollows of Odessa's face, sunken cheeks and sunken temples and deep, deep eyes. The lids on her eyes were thin as onion skin, half-closed; and her flesh was dry like parchment; and the body that was once strapping now resembled broomsticks in her bed -- skinny arms on a caved stomach, fingers as long as chalk."

Minute details, lengthy physical descriptions, a sensitivity to the unique characteristics of each human so that the reader does not feel alienated by the story but is drawn into it, and yet -- each of these unique, sometimes bizarre characters eventually reflects the universal truths about humans, themselves and the readers. Wangerin's watchful serendipity discerns in the most powerless character the working of God and the possible teaching that God can bring to each of us through these unexpected sources.

And many of these characters that he creates are childlike or learn to become childlike in the course of the work. "Unless you turn and become like children, you will never enter the kingdom of heaven." And his characters learn their powerlessness, learn to trust their heavenly Father, and learn to love, laugh and respond to life with childlike wonder and excitement. As he states in his work, <u>Little Lamb, Who make Thee</u>, "Give us, Oh Lord, clear eyes, uncomplicated hearts, and guileless tongues. Make us children again!

"When we are wide-eyed children the world is filled with things both visible and invisible...and we laughed without embarrassment; and could gasp with delight at a sudden, beautiful thing, and our loving was given immediate expression; we accepted forgiveness completely...and because of that we were fearless...Oh sisters and brothers (so often so teenish in spite of our years because we desire the approval of our peers), if we would turn and become like little children, then fearless and faithful contemplation of the gravest mysteries need never end for us.

No, not ever: for it is as little children
that we shall enter the kingdom of heaven."

Thus, Wangerin through his works reveals to us, sometimes through strange, uneducated, childlike characters, the pathway out of childishness and self-centeredness, teenagehood and its desire for acceptance, and adult one-sided realism, and into child-likeness and relaxation in the arms of God. And to learn to sleep in these strong arms of God's, "to sleep now, child, in perfect peace. You are God's -- and he spreads his wings above you now." And to show this journey to childlikeness and to enable the reader to experience his/her own journey, Wangerin brings his characters through selfishness, hurt, suffering, the death of the old self, and to the rebirth and knowledge of ourselves as vulnerable children in the arms of a loving Father. As he emphasizes as he retells the Parable of the Prodigal Son, the Father is waiting for us to come home to him, standing on the rooftop watching for us and longing to embrace us and comfort us. And because of this belief Wangerin ends <u>The Book of Sorrows</u> in this way: "Chauntecleer seems to shrink, curling in on himself...Then helplessly, he bursts into tears...Chauntecleer is gulping air and sobbing like an infant...So Ferric Coyote pulls his own poor body forward until he is next to the Rooster. Then like a mother and a newborn, he begins to lick Chauntecleer, stroke and stroke and stroke, beak and neck and back and breast, washing him clean of the Winter's filth -- and smiling...And Pertelote rocked her husband, gazing toward the nighttime coming from the East." And at the end of <u>The Crying for a Vision</u> the mighty, conquering warrior, Fire Thunder, "makes a strange nasal sound, an astonishing sound, a baby's whine...Poor Fire Thunder! He made a mewing sound in his nose...The man threw down his ax and started to wail in that shrill voice which children use when they are lost...And then we saw Fire Thunder crumpled down to the ground and begin to cry. 'Hownh, hownh,' he wept. And we saw that his shoulders were shaking with the sobs. And we, too, perhaps because we were all so tired, so tired -- we were crying too...Fire Thunder wrapped his arms around himself and rocked back and forth crying..." And in <u>The Orphean Passages</u> Pastor Orpheus is also brought to his rebirth and childlikeness through his suffering. "But when he (Orpheus) did move, he felt something beneath his head. He turned and touched it, then his heart swelled up, and Orpheus started to cry...'Don't cry,' said the man's soft voice.

> "'But let him,' said the woman's delighted
> voice... 'All God's children got to cry.'

Orpheus felt a hand on his cheek then looked and saw a dark form crouched beside him. He took the hand and held it...'I love you,' said Coral Jones swiftly, nervously. 'And God loves you too. He didn't never not love you. No, but he's been waitin' for you, been waitin' ever' day of your life, to call you his child.'"

In the same way, as Wangerin recounts a moment with one of his parishioners Miz Lil, he states that he starts crying,

> "and suddenly Miz Lil's hand is on my knee.
>
> "'Pastor, why are you crying?'
>
> "For just a moment the darkness in Lillian
> Lander's living room is an amnesty, and it doesn't
> matter that I speak with appeal, like a child and not
> like a Pastor. 'Is God,' I plead, 'Miz Lil -- is God smil-
> ing -- is he smiling on me?'"

And those characters who speak the words of childlike wisdom to us through his works are described in childlike terms: "Odessa Williams says to the children in her room: 'An whenever you sing, I'm going to be with you still. An' you know how I can say such a miraculous thing? Why cause we in Jesus,' she whispered in mystery. 'Babies, babies, we be in the hand of Jesus, old ones, young ones, and us and all you together. Jesus he hold us in his hand.'" Pastor Wangerin states also in "Baby Hannah," "And even now the maternal God remembers my delivery. I am not lost in the multitudes...What Mother doesn't whisper the baby's name, remembering? So God loves me and calls me by name." And his son Matthew, at the age of eight, "opens a door in the universe and through my son and in my face. The Glory of the Lord had burst from a little child. Not Sunday School lessons, nor all the sermons he had heard nor preached...but Jesus Christ himself was the cause of this most dramatic and real wonder. Matthew didn't speak the Christ; for an instant Matthew was the Christ, and I saw it; not with my eyes, for that was his own short fingered hand on my knee, but with my soul...Even so did Jesus reveal himself and sign my soul."

So Wangerin's characters may be children, inner-city poor, street people. But they all become the vehicles through whom God can speak, and they all can be the messengers of God to us if we are "watchful of the particularities of the interactions in our lives and are willing to suspend our adult disbelief and guardedness." Then if we can be "sensitive to God -- as children are -- God, like the hero in an old play, will constantly burst onto the scenes of our lives."

All of Wangerin's characters echo his cry: "No, I will not see the scene (of the nativity) with an empirical, modern eye. I refuse to accept the narrow sophistications and dead-eyed adulthoods of a 'realistic' world. I choose to stay a child...I will paint my picture with baby awe, wide-eyed, primitive, and faithful...And I will call it true; for it sees what is but not seen. It makes the invisible obvious."

Wangerin's stories describe the veiled existence of "adulthood with its facts and rationality, and the unveiled world of God, where he is bright and present and active and loving"...And both of these worlds become real to the reader as he/she experiences them in his stories, and the "latter existence gives meaning to the former." And their stories reflect our stories, and we are enabled to see the invisible elements of our own existence which we have failed to notice for so long, and we begin to dare to risk becoming children once again so that we can experience the Father's love without the knowing of adults that is "troubled by extraneous thoughts." And perhaps, if we truly hear the maturity of his Christian vision, in us "the best of the child will continue and the best of adulthood will emerge, and we will be able to love more quickly, more spontaneously and with less confusion, and be fearless in our childlike faith because we also accept God's love and forgiveness as children."

"This, then, is the sequence of my knowing of my God...I move to the sweet embrace of the Savior -- and then the cosmos has a cradle quality, and I lie down, and I am a babe therein. Here in my 50th year I have become the child whom creation holds, whom God consoles with lullabies, the praise of angels and the music of the spheres."

Chapter III.

WANGERIN'S
VISION OF GOD

Shaping our lives with Words of Power

WANGERIN'S
VISION OF GOD

"Stories are rainbows in which the totality of experience appears temporarily to our consciousness before it fades. It always comes after conflict, and it remains just long enough in our view to remind us all is well and that it will return but only after more threatening conflict." (Lacota Story Telling)

"How long do we go in the memory of our sweet experience of Jesus...The experience happens, truly does happen...but always one thing follows: Time...And what do we have? The memory - whose reality is in the past. And the memory is of a promise - whose reality is in the future. But we are in the present." (The Orphean Passages)

"In a sharp, sweet stab of pain, the shadow of the ghost of Jesus appears - there, there so lovely as to take our breath away. Oh, but he is so beautiful!

"But in the instant that we become aware that we are seeing him, he vanishes from our sight...Having seen him once, and cherishing the picture, we are a thousand times hungrier to see him again." (The Orphean Passages)

Wangerin's vision of God is one in which sorrow and joy, fear and hope, death and resurrection, rebuke and forgiveness are all intermixed. And since he believes that it is in "hearing that faith begins," he retells the Christian story in many forms so that those who read his stories may truly "hear" the story of Christ.

"Is it in hearing that faith begins? Yes. And is faith an intimate, real relationship with Jesus? Yes. And this is the strength of our sacred story, that when we hear it, we experience it, and in this experience we meet the Christ, and him whom we meet in the extremes, of his love, we most likewise love." (Reliving the Passion, p. 12) Without the story of Christ as the foundational truth of his writing, Wangerin could rightly be accused of overwriting or sentimentalism, despair or Pollyanna optimism. But all of his works and the emotions he displays in them reflect the ultimate truths of the Christian faith and, therefore, give hope and significance to the reader. And since to be "in faith is to be changing, and our apprehension of God is in relationship and is, therefore, dramatic, his works reflect the growth and progress and stories of the Christian attempting to love this God who has revealed himself through Christ, and Wangerin constantly shows the experiential aspect of our faith -- that which we desire so much, yet "sometimes in our lives only vaguely see," and he enables us to see the workings of God in the everyday moments of our lives.

Wangerin defines the faithing journey in The Orphean Passages in the following way:

"Faith-flux. Faith flows. To be in faith is to be changing...To be in faith is ever to be moving through the passages of faith, and to be moved by them. It must be a verb, then: faithing. And three things cry the change of it:

1. That it is relationship, as I have said, which manifests its life in change and which, to be, must also still be changing.

2. That it is relationship -- with the living God, whose life against ours, mercifully, gracefully, changes. Faithing is the constant losing of one's balance, the constant falling forward (which is required even for so common a locomotion as walking.) It is the constant loss of stability, the denying one's self and dying unto God; unto God Jahweh; unto a Who and not a What.

3.That it is relationship with the living God - enacted in this world, this world of the furious swirl, in which all things flow...It is the unspeakable love of God that he comes to meet us in the very terms of this world."

But in Wangerin's vision the "world has grown dark in this present age, and that's a fact. The cold of human hurt wails around us, and hunger is a whiteout, and hatreds make a blizzard, and we've but a shack to hide in." ("Little Children, Can You Tell?") But these facts, although many times forming the events of Wangerin's stories, do not cause him to limit his works to "facts, nothing but facts," for it is in the very midst of chaos and darkness that we most need stories, and especially the story of God in Christ breaking through our darkness. As he states:

"Let 'realists' scorn our story. Let them sing that it does not stand a secular scrutiny. Its consequences do! For we will go on telling it; and we, dazzled children, will take our places with it, meeting Jesus when we do. And then the warmth and hope and the peace of this Truth will beam from our beings as evidence most empirical, real enough to heat the realist through the night to the dawn and the sunrise..."

Wangerin's vision of God cannot understand those who would diminish the central story of Christ into just one of many myths or into something more relevant, for "If we don't have a higher truth to offer the world, then who are we?...Without Jesus we are nothing." And so his stories become holy things reflecting the truth of the one who originally names us: Jesus Christ the righteous. Not that he always uses Christian symbols or words (as his The Crying for a Vision shows), but he is always true to the reality of the Christian faith. His image of humans is rooted in his deep belief in the Christian revelation: "We are severed from God, and this severance makes us dead in trespasses and sin. This remains our mortal condition, but this, precisely, we spend extraordinary funds of energy trying to deny." Thus, it may take some of the secondary dyings to bring us to our limits since Wangerin believes that faith never springs from personal strength or overweening self-esteem. "No, out of personal weakness faith reaches to a God of strength, out of failure and need and self-doubt...And he who has cried, 'I can't' might better than others hear the Almighty murmur: 'But I can.'" (Mourning into Dancing)

But to bring us to this point of weakness, of reaching out to God, God, in his gracious love, "begins to reveal unto us such treacheriness and threats in the world that we know we must die soon...The first act of Divine love is to persuade us of the reality of death...But we need to suffer extremely to know our extreme need." And, according to Wangerin, every secondary dying, precisely by the grief that it causes us, is a call to a deeper truth and a means by which we might return to the Lord. "That is the goodness of painful grief: to teach us our need again, and to turn us to God. What are these secondary deaths that God uses in his severe mercy to bring us to the end of ourselves so that we become like children and learn to trust him again?

"1. Separation from one another in our relationships (divorces, betrayals, gossip, abandonment.)
2. Separation from our natural environment (futility of labor, natural disasters, ecological crisis, physical deaths.)
3. Separation from ourselves (hatred of self, loss of physical abilities, death of dreams, failure, guilt.)

All of these secondary deaths are means through which the "righteous execution of the sinner by the gracious will of God will occur...The death of everything the person clings to that prevents his loving God shall come, and it shall occur in the arena of the world." We literally are brought to see our extreme weaknesses so that we reach out to God.

These beliefs concerning the spiritual journey of the faithing one form the basis of Wangerin's realistic seriousness and emphasis upon loneliness, death, severance of relationships and sin. But these are absolutely necessary to Wangerin so that resurrection and trust and love of God can occur. Without the dyings we would never know the resurrection and its glory. And in Wangerin's writings, the joy, cosmos, and relationship with God which occur are emphasized as much as the separations and death, so that the whole of the Christian message is heard and experienced, not just a part of it.

Chapter IV.

LIVING IN THE *IS*

Shaping our lives with Words of Power

LIVING IN THE *IS*

One of the general themes that is behind most of Wangerin's thinking is the need for self-knowledge and self-reflection, even if this is painful, and a need to remember the past, even if one wishes to forget one's past, so one can truly live in the present. Only through remembering and repenting of past sins can we be forgiven, healed, and matured. But remembering the past can also hinder our progress if we refuse to accept the healing and the growth God offers and go on to being raised to life again. We will remember it, "it shall never pass away. Something lingers (from past sorrows), it shall never be quite forgotten -- nor shall the grieving ever altogether pass away. Something lingers...and those who are comforted and forgiven look at life with new eyes...and we are humbled as never before."

But most of us, according to Wangerin, never face our past and accept the healing for it that God offers, for we mourn over it, feel ashamed about it, constantly try to atone for it. And others of us never live in the present because we are always looking to the future, waiting for "tomorrow to change everything." And we never learn trust and hope, and we never enjoy the present. We don't live in the "now, now." Wangerin illustrates these concepts in The Book of the Dunn Cow: "But, yes. As a matter of fact, since the war was done, and the earth closed, Chauntecleer had wanted to forget Mundo Cani, because there is guilt in such a memory. The Dog's good act ever stood in accusation of the Rooster's sinfulness. Chauntecleer did not like to think of himself as a failure at the final moment. Therefore, Chauntecleer did not like to think of Mundo Cani at all.

"And that strangely is why he was willing to talk about Mundo Cani to anyone, to praise him vigorously.

"So Pertelote had not one problem but two: one whose present was too much steeped in the past, and one whose present denied the past altogether."

It is difficult for us to have an appropriate response to our past, and we need to understand how thoroughly our past controls us and how long it takes to learn to accept it, be healed of it, learn from it and be resurrected to new life.

"'You can't help thinking of the past,' Pertelote said. 'And you are not, Chauntecleer, able to clean out of your soul the thing that has changed you. Do pity the Weasel. He's slower with the changes than you are. He needed the past and its order more than you...'"

But Chauntecleer responds: "'As long as he remembers in this way, as long as he sulks, he's a memory for me of what happened. I'm going to forget the past, Pertelote, And if I have to forget John Wesley with it -- well, so. That's the way it is.'"

But by the end of The Book of Sorrows, the Animals have learned to live in the present appropriately:

"But nobody wept. The time of weeping was over. They knew better now. They knew to say *Is* and *Was* in righteous separation, to sit in the *Is*, to remember the *Was*, and themselves merely to be..."

And as Chauntecleer dies he can remember his sons and Mundo Cani with affection and humor, and order is once again restored to the Animal's universe. As Pertelote states: "'This is what I have thought that under the everlasting stars all time is short, and the length of it is foolish to measure. *Is* is enough to say. And *Was* is a fine enough memory when it is done.' She hugged her husband close to her throat, 'Right Chauntecleer?' There spread a smile across his beak, though his eyes stayed closed. 'I hear you, woman,' he said.

"John Wesley said, 'Wee Widow Mouse, she was.'

"'Right,' said Pertelote. 'As lovely a *Was* as any of us can expect to have. Cherish it, John.'

"'And Rachel,' said Ferric Coyote. 'And little Benomi the oldest Coyote.'"

"Pertelote nodded peacefully, saying, 'Right, right. Keep them close to you.'"

Only through a proper remembering of the past can we sing in the present and live in faith and trust, with gratitude to God. So in <u>The Book of Sorrows</u>, "Pertelote can lift up her voice and begin to sing on the battlefield. She sang as if she walked the rim of the universe, like the Moon, a pale and lovely presence everywhere on the earth."

Grief and the remembering of it also enable us to become children again and to be held in the bosom of Jesus and be comforted. But as Wangerin states in <u>Mourning into Dancing</u>, "Not every time a person grieves will he be brought to deeper faith by the experience. But he might....We are all the boy who clings to the tree branch afraid to drop into his Father's arms to safety, clinging to our idealized view of the world....We spend a long time screaming No!...But, always, God is present. God has always been present." But as we remember the past and its griefs, it is difficult to remember in such a way that we learn trust.

As Gloria learns when she loses her beloved Sonny Boy: "After church Gloria lingered in the pew -- praying, I thought. She hath ever been a mighty assaulter of heaven....As I walked up the aisle to my tiny study, she said, 'Pastor?

"I turned into her pew and sat. .

She was quiet a while, gazing toward the Altar.

There stood upon it a tall brass crucifix. Above that, filled with Southern sunlight, was a stained window in which Jesus knelt at a stone, praying in Gethsemene.

She said softly, 'I been knowin' Jesus since I was little-bitty. And I have loved him. And I have called upon him. Why did I hurt so badly when Sonny Boy died? Why does it take me so long, so long. I mean my whole life long until now --'

She fell silent again.

'What is the matter with me? Don't I really believe?'

There was much that I didn't say aloud that morning.

I didn't say: 'It takes the poor adult forever to become a child again, able to make her bed in the bosom of Jesus.'

I didn't say: 'We resist falling completely and helplessly into his arms. Helplessness scares us. We wish to keep a little control. The lack of it looks so bad.'"

But according to Wangerin, when we do face our past griefs and in humbleness release them into the arms of Jesus and refuse to maintain our own stability by our own righteousness, strength or control, "the relationship which God had intended from the beginning of time, full and free between himself and you, he now renews. He who catches you, keeps you. And then we can say with God, 'For this my daughter was lost and is found; she was dead and is alive. Somebody run out and kill the fatted calf, and let's have a party.'"

Thus, in all of Wangerin's works, the characters need to face their past, take responsibility for their errors, and in humbleness give control to God so that they can live in the "eternal now" fully involved in the "isness of life." Thus, Pastor Orpheus learns to live in the Is and can pray in perfect peace, quietly, straight into the ear of Jesus. "There were no distances any more between himself and his Lord because this rental house was where Jesus lived," and in our own lives "the gospel no longer will seem irrelevant or unreal but, as for Pastor Orpheus so for us, Christ becomes a continuing ally and a holy destroyer of death."

And "Miz Lil" can laugh again after her husband's death and remember him with love. And as she does, "Silence comes down upon us like (I say) a double portion of the Spirit -- and with the silence, the mantle on the shoulder of the ancient prophetess." And Pertelote can sing compline again for the Animals with a voice like an angel. Even Fire Thunder's past is redeemed by Waskn Mani's sacrifice so that he can dance to the drumbeat of the earth again and "hold the infant in his arms, brushing the snow from her cheek, and she (the infant) can look in his good eye and suck his thumb for comfort."

All of these characters, just like each of us as followers of Christ, need to have their pasts forgiven and healed so that they can live in the daily reality of Christ's presence, and in each of them we see our own spiritual and human yearnings reflected so that we too can learn to end the time of self-righteousness, control, hurt, and weeping for the time of weeping is over. We know better now. We "know to say *Is* and *Was* in righteous separation, to sit in the *Is*, to remember the *Was*, and ourselves merely to be."

Learning to be and to be healed of the past and to trust God with the future enables one to manifest one of the highest truths of the Christian faith, according to Wangerin: "Learning in love to lay down one's life for another just as Christ sacrificed himself for each of us. Love is the willing ability to sacrifice oneself for the sake of another. It is the sacrifice that is observable. It is the sacrifice that validates the truth of a true religion, for sacrifice remains a riddle to the world except it be explained by faith. At the core of Christianity...is the cross of Christ, his love made manifest in sacrifice." ("What is Hell?", p. 7)

And this sacrifice involves many areas for the individual, for we not only lay down our physical lives for one another, not only die to the old self to be renewed in Christ, not only sacrifice our dreams for another, but we lay down the events of our lives...and "humble ourselves so that we make of ourselves a parable... Doctrine may judge the rightness of my perceptions...but I stand before you in flesh and blood; I risk the disclosure of myself and my experiences: I present you with the very stuff itself of the events which have shaped this person's life before you, and so reveal the Shaper shaping." ("Preaching," p. 76)

But many times in our lives we don't recognize or notice the sacrifices either of others or of Christ himself. As he asks: "Then why haven't we been astounded by such holiness? Well, I think we are by nature blind to sacrifice...Perhaps we have to suffer sacrifice in order to understand it." So instead of explaining sacrifice to us in his works, Wangerin tells us stories so that we experience the depth of sacrifice and thus become aware of its holiness and grace. And the sacrifices which occur in Wangerin's works are voluntary on the part of the sacrificer, just as Christ's death and sacrifice were voluntary. As he states when he realizes his children's needs and chose to sacrifice for them. "Then when I chose, when I sacrificed the writer-self and consciously renounced my book and offered my children, completely, a parent, I had to do the former to allow the latter. These were the same act after all. I had to let the core of me die -- for a while at least, that they might properly live..." (Little Lamb Who Made Thee?, p. 137) And so Wangerin also sees many mothers making the same sacrifice. "There came for you (as a mother) a moment of conscious, sacred sacrifice. In that moment the self of yourself became a smoke, and the smoke went up to heaven as a perpetual prayer for the sake of your children.

"And when it is a voluntary sacrifice, it is no less than divine."

The fact of the necessity of sacrifice and its holiness in God's universe is found throughout Wangerin's works. In The Book of the Dunn Cow, Mundo Cani chooses to give his life for the other Animals:

"'He went down and it should have been me.'
'Oh, Chauntecleer. He knew he had to go down.
Don't you understand that? There was never any
question about who would make the sacrifice.'"

And at the end of <u>The Book of Sorrows</u>, Ferric Coyote sacrifices himself for Chauntecleer, to offer him forgiveness; and in
<u>Branta and the Golden Stone</u>, Branta becomes a goose and sacri-
fices herself to allow the other geese to live.

But Wangerin's longest treatment of this theme is in his work
<u>The Crying for a Vision</u>. The need to atone for sin by an act of
sacrifice runs through the story. As Virginia Owens states in
"Walter Wangerin and the Cosmic Equation": "There is yet a
third article of faith inherent in Wangerin's stories. This ongoing
savage operation we call sacrifice is both necessary for the survival of the world and efficacious...And those who have to pay
the price for sin are often not those who inflicted the damage. In
other words, life's not fair. The innocent suffer; the virtuous are
sacrificed...the deficit can be made up only by a worthy sacrifice;
a grandmother's life devoted to raising her grandchildren in the
place of a drug-addicted parent, the humble Mundo Cani, not the
proud Chauntecleer, losing his life confronting Wyrm...So in <u>The
Crying for a Vision</u>, an orphaned Lacota boy becomes the sacrifice, not the proud Fire Thunder."

The depth of this sacrifice is explained by Waskn Mani's
Grandmother:

> "Waskn Mani, listen to me; my death did not do
> any good for anyone. No one took benefit from my
> dying because I did not give it away. I fought it! I
> fought dying all the way to the end...But I was dead;
> I loved no one...
>
> But you have a choice, boy. Waskn Mani, you are
> the same as I was before my dying. The pain in you is
> your love for the people...
>
> But you, Waskn Mani, if you choose the death
> that is at the end of the loving before it kills the peo-
> ple, if you choose a willing sacrifice, if one person
> should die in the place of the people - well, then they
> all might have the benefit. The people might live."

And as Moves Walking willingly gives his life to save his people, Fire Thunder is forced to ask for his life: "And Fire Thunder said softly: 'Moves Walking, do you give your life that the people may live?' As the Mountain looked down upon Fire Thunder, and the light grew warmer around him, the boy said, 'Yes, I do. I do.'"

Wangerin believes that to sacrifice one for another is one of the central truths of the universe and that it reflects Christ's sacrifice for the sins of each person. "For if death defines us, so that we who came from nothing also go back to nothing, then death is a worm that curls inside our every act...But the Creator God put a cross in the center of human history -- to be the center, ever....Now, therefore, it is the person and the passion of Jesus Christ which defines us....Behold, this is the central event of all human history."

"Here is the paradox, both impossible and true. Jesus is rejected by God, is cut off completely from God, is hung on a tree and thereby cursed...And yet: it is in this same Jesus, at the same moment, precisely because of his sacrifice and death, that God is most present to the world. In Christ's sacrifice we received life, and as we sacrifice ourselves for one another we enable them to experience this new life in Christ also....We literally have been crucified with Christ, yet we live, but not us, but Christ lives in us, and the life we now live we live by faith in the Son of God who loved us and gave himself for us."

As Wangerin states regarding a retired Lutheran missionary: "He has with calm conviction preached to a Muslim tribe called the Fulani that the highest truth and the clearest revelation of God is to be seen in Christ the crucified....We must not be ashamed of genuine selfless love and the Holy Word which purges both the body and the soul of their diseases." Or as Nelson affirms: "If we don't have a higher truth (as Christians) to offer the world, then who are we?...Without Jesus, we are nothing." ("Ashamed of Jesus?", p. 5)

So Wangerin's writings reflect this deep faith and its central message of sacrifice, grace and atonement through Christ. "An artist of faith -- a real artist! -- may therefore cry: Listen, we have a myth that consoles us, one worthy of a lasting belief, one we can surely live by. It is 'myth' insofar as it is the timeless defining story by which we make sense of a senseless existence. But it is truth insofar as it happened. It is vaster than I am (says the artist). I did not create it; it created me. I may name it with my words; but it is the word which named me first: Jesus Christ the righteous."

And Wangerin uses his powerful words and his stories to name this Jesus to the readers so that they can experience his truths not merely know them. "I tell you of Arthur Forte, and behold! God is in the squalor...God shaping me like a clay pot...I tell you of the day my Matthew forgave me, and Jesus Christ walks through the doors of one man's study, to ease his burning guilt in the cool blood of the cross...the stories of experiences (themselves becoming experiences for the hearers) prepare the people to see God approach them through experience...Out of experience rises the Word in order to lodge in experience once again. And story is experience communicated." (The Ragman, p. 76)

Chapter V.

WANGERIN'S THEORIES OF NATURE

Shaping our lives with Words of Power

WANGERIN'S
THEORIES OF NATURE

"Signs! Signs! The world is a book.
And what is not the writing?
The world is charged for them that look
With grandeur, God's reminding
In all things near to thee
    To read and see
    Divinity.
And signs explode for thee
Epiphanies.
Epiphanies."

Wendell Berry

Wangerin's works contain many myths concerning nature and many minute observations of the natural world, for this world being a creation of God and the place of Christ's incarnation, is validated in these events as important to us as God's children. Not only do we have the responsibility to maintain the world but we also have the ability to see God's miracles and to hear his voice in the natural world.

And throughout his works and because of his unique "watchfulness of particularities," Wangerin reveals these epiphanies to the reader and allows the reader to see the world charged with the "grandeur of God." As he states concerning his own spiritual journey: "This, then, is the sequence of my knowing of my God: first I am the Gentile in Romans 1:20 to whom the creation of the world reveals the eternal power and deity of God. Isness persuades me that God is. But then I am the disciple who finds in the face of Jesus what sort of God God is, forgiving and merciful and kind.

Thus, I move from the primal awe of the Creator to the sweet embrace of the Savior -- and then the cosmos has a cradle quality, and I lie down, and I am a babe therein. Here in my 50th year I have become the child whom creation holds, whom God consoles with lullabies, the praise of angels, and the music of the spheres." ("Turning Fifty," p. 7)

And Wangerin urges his readers through his fictional and his non-fictional works to learn to be watchful and to listen to God through this natural revelation. "Once, years ago," wrote Wangerin, "I surprised my sons by crying: 'Look! That tree is your sister!' I was feeling spasms of kinship in my chest...But how do I convince my boys of this wonder?

> And how do I convince you that all natural things are beings worthy of our love and honor since they are, as we are, the handiwork of God, whose breathing sustains us all? How do I cause you to rejoice in the union of all life in all its forms?"

This wonder and awe and a feeling of kinship with nature pervades all of Wangerin's works, but he is careful not to equate God with his creation: "No, nature is not to be worshiped. And humanity is unique, surely, the emblem of the Deity in creation, God's image here and the object of his holy love (if not always of holy contentment and pride.)" But this distinction does not lessen our kinship with and love for nature, for if "this sense of kinship is lost, or benumbed in us, or else scorned as a silly sentimentalizing of reality, then creation is made vulnerable also to our unique sinning, and we shall (and we do) destroy without remorse the things that God has placed in our care for the tilling and the keeping and the naming thereof." ("The Canticle of the Sun," p. 6)

But most of us in our fast-paced and rational culture have forgotten our proper relationship to nature, have failed to hear God's voice in the natural universe, and have lost our childlike sense of wonder and awe at the beauty and magnificence of God's world. So Wangerin constantly reminds us in his works of our kinship with nature, reveals to us God's grandeur in the natural world, and urges us to experience for ourselves the childlike wonder and joy we daily miss as we casually fail to notice or to appreciate the created world. And we destroy or ignore this creation of God.

Quoting from Wendell Berry's poem in Sabbaths, Wangerin

writes: "This is as rich a picture of worship as I have ever read. And I am invited to join! But the trees are not, as the holiness was not, mere metaphor. They are trees. You and I (with every young Baptist preacher Wendell carried to the woods) are invited to worship with trees, creatures of God, humble and pristine in obedience: 'Apostles of the living light.'" And he continues: "Dear Christians, within so holy a kinship, how can we foul the friend we walk on? How can we destroy the rivers, transgress the trees, murder the earth with greed and sinning? Too many people and corporate gluttons obey nothing but their hungers at the expense of the rest of creation. They walk as though they were gods the trees must worship, before whom the land must sacrifice itself. Their footprints are destruction. In contrast, we should recognize that

> 'In Fall their brightened leaves, released
> Fly down the wind, and we are pleased
> To walk on radiance, amazed.
> O light come down to earth, be praised.'"

Although Wangerin sees many people sinning against God's creation, tossing "fast food wrappers on the highway, tossing beer cans in the river, tossing trash -- the detritus of your burned out desire, the soul you use and lose -- wherever others don't see you," and stating as a group of high schoolers did when he talked to them about the natural environment - "So what? It doesn't matter what I do," he finds a few who recognize the importance of a respect for God's creation; and these are the ones he uses as his objective correlatives for his readers. As he states in "The Eye of the Farmer": "At eighty-eight he (Martin Buhlmann) doesn't talk much, nor did he ever...But his spirit knows the holiness of God's creation, and though he doesn't say it...you can see...that this farmer stands on the earth with reverence." As Wangerin watches this farmer (his Father-in-law) "watch the earth," he states, "Humbly he loved what he looked at. He, with the Lord and the soil, stood in union. All was holy; when I beheld the farmer's reverence, I knew it too....He and the farmers like him preserve in their very being the truth which we, in our sinful ignorance, have forgotten: that we belong to the earth, and the earth belongs to God. These are holy, living dependencies, as necessary as blood to flesh....I plead that we live on this earth with reverence."

Others, like these farmers, also have not forgotten our relationship to the earth, but many times, these are the very ones that culture ignores or calls "retarded." As Wangerin states regarding Dorothy, his Sister-in-law who has Downs Syndrome: "Retarded? Hardly! This woman has an apprehension of the universe more intimate and more devout than my own. Her knowing isn't troubled by extraneous thought...I've been to Holden thrice before; but now I saw it for the first time, with primal eyes because of Dorothy. She is the quick one. My responses are slow and baffled....I, in the high, green crown of God - in simple creation - was the retarded one. How often we get it backward! How much we miss when we do!" ("Dorothy - the Crown of God") And as he writes in another article: "You (Dorothy) love the things of God as God loves them...you pause to cry at beauty...Dorothy, you are the image of God in my world!" ("The Retarded? The Image of God," p. 5)

And in others Wangerin sees this same quality, even in an inner-city cop: "That which you had you cherished....Therefore, an afternoon at the edge of a sleepy water was no less than Eden prepared especially for you....I miss you, Arthur Bias!...I miss the assurance that fishing's enough, that this afternoon sunlight is surely enough...Oh, Arthur, maybe you were, in your ordinariness, extraordinary -- a cop who caused harmony! A friend who, in fishing, hooked God at the heart."

With the above reverence for nature, it is not surprising that in Wangerin's novel, <u>The Crying for a Vision</u>, Wangerin in the Lacota people found the perfect symbol through which to express not only his Christian truths about redemption and salvation, but also the truths concerning our relationship to the world God has created and placed us in. For he believes "that in the Lacota any people may see itself. In them, in the clean, uncomplicated knowledge which the Lacota achieved concerning themselves and their relationship to the whole created world.

> "In them: not only in their culture, which through many generations learned the plains, and loved the buffalo and lived in union with nature red and blue; not only in their history, which sent them west before there were ponies, then gave them ponies and therein swiftness and distance and glory...I have found in the Lacota vision a rich analogue for the relationship any people of genuine faith experiences with creation and

the Creator....therefore, it was my artistic choice to use their world as the controlling metaphor of the novel."

And in this novel, we clearly experience the relationship with creation and the Creator which many of us as Christians have lost, or many times may never have had, and which we need if we are to worship God as intended. "He (Waskn Mani) felt so happy to be in the center of all these circles; the fires first; then the people whose sweat-scent and sage gave him comfort and whose laughter he loved with his whole heart; next the circle of tipis like silent guards around them; then trees of the forest, murmuring, nodding at the tops of them; and then forever and ever the plains. The earth. The sky. All." And we the readers are urged throughout this work to

> "Wachin ksapo yo. (Pay attention)...Be attentive, boy. Pay attention to every living thing because anything might be carrying the news of heaven down to you. Anything!....Wachin ksapo yo. Be attentive. Even an ant can tell the truth, but who would know this if first he does not listen to the ant."

And nature does speak to us of our Creator God and, according to Wangerin, nature is quicker to praise God than we are. And although "Springtime is not the source of our creed of Resurrection, it is the arena for Christ's resurrection...and in spring the whole creation is not groaning. Right now (in spring) creation does not travail in pain. For a little while creation is eager with life and bursting with hope....Dear Christian, this is more than a poet's metaphor. This is the truth of God writ large in nature. This is the conjoining of the worlds, spiritual and natural. For if our sin could cause creation to grieve beneath a curse, God's mercy can relieve the grief and the curse awhile and so make manifest God's redemption....Spiritually speaking, God saved us by the dying in Christ...Although the effect was wonderfully spiritual, the world in which Christ rose was emphatically this one: air and soil and rivers and streams and trees -- and the jonquil! In Christ the whole of creation has proof of redemption, both we and nature together; but nature is quicker to praise, more obedient to reflect, profounder, grander, more faithful to demonstrate the certitude of that redemption."

So in The Crying for a Vision, sin can break the "circle of the world and when the hoop is broken everything suffers. Everything...Every creature is appointed to serve another. That's the hocaka, the sacred hoop. If someone for selfishness ceases to serve, the circle breaks and creatures go hungry...when everyone suffers the world itself may die....Well, if the sacred hoop is not repaired, everyone dies. This is the end of the world. But the hoop may be repaired if someone will give his life for the sin." So in this work one must choose to sacrifice his life to save the world, and this reflects God's sacrifice for us to save us, to break the bondage of sin and to free creation from the curse of sin.

In all of his works, Wangerin reveals an intimate relationship with nature, and encourages us to see creation with new eyes and to listen to God's still small voice in his world. "But, as he states, there is a better voice to argue the union we all have with all of creation, one better to sing of the love that springs from this union back unto the Creator: Francis of Assisi. Francis, whose poverty abolished divisions between himself and God's more primal gifts of nature (Monies and marketings, you see, possessions, ambitions and the enlargement of barns all tend to deaden our love for the wheat within them) - Francis, I say, whose life directly encountered the creatures of God - sang this song:

'Be Thou praised, my Lord, above all the creatures
     of Brother Sun, who gives the day and lightens
     us therewith...
Be Thou praised, my Lord, of Sister Moon and the
     stars; in the heaven hast thou formed them, clear
     and precise and comely...
Be Thou praised, my Lord, of Brother Wind and of
     air, and the cloud, and of fair and all weather, by
     which Thou givest to Thy creatures sustenance...
Be Thou praised, O my Lord, of our Sister Mother
     Earth, which sustains and hath us in rule, and
     produces divers fruits with colored flowers and
     herbs.'"

And what should our response be as Christians, if we recognize the truths of our relationship with the earth and all of God's creation? According to Wangerin, "God distributes every natural thing as a gift, an abiding sign of love for those who use and delight in it....What then?...Why then, any time we break the harmonious relationships of all things created by God, we have broken it to steal.

"A dying river is a theft. A thing was stolen from God. And countless benefits, all intentions of the Creator, were stolen from countless creatures large and small....Then I set myself over the Deity, denying God's decisions by revising them. Moreover my one act rips the network of God's 1000 acts, destroying more than I can imagine, since every gift of the Creator is inwoven with all creation! Then, the things that seem in my possession are actually in my care. My care!" ("Thou Shalt Not Steal," p. 7)

Or as he asks in "The Eye of the Farmer": "What do we think it means that God gave us 'dominion' over creation? That we own it? That we can bend it to our own desires? That the earth is merely a resource by which we support and satisfy ourselves? Hardly! In the beginning, because we ourselves were included in God's image, our dominion was meant to image God's sovereignty over creation and not our own. We were God's emblem, steward, servant. We were placed here to serve God by serving the earth and so to be served by it. The earth is alive: It can die. The earth is holy, owned by God. Know it as holy, a trust to us, and then we will not kill it but keep it, and it will keep our children."

But if we sin against the earth and dominate it by selfishly using it to satisfy ourselves, we will watch the earth die and experience the loneliness felt by the Lacota in The Crying for a Vision:

"This was the start of the year of terrible hunger and loneliness. And maybe the loneliness was worse than the hunger...The Lacota missed the sounds and the smell and the presence of the animals. All human people began to feel solitary in the universe. Strangers. No wolf packs howled in the black winter's night. No one barked. No one sang the first birdsong. Crickets were gone. The little tree frogs did not call to one another. The evening did not talk. The night did not peep or chirp or rasp the insects' melody in ancient rhythm. Silence lay like a mountain on the heart of the Lacota...

It was an empty land. A dead land. They sky was high and dry, a brilliant far away blue. The hot wind did not cease blowing. The grass rattled like small bones, the air smelled of serpents' skins, the earth cracked. The earth herself was dying."

But, according to Wangerin, we can choose to be proper stewards of God's earth, to love and respect his creation, and like Johnny Appleseed, choose to leave a blessing behind for future generations. "Insofar as we love the earth, we feed the future. That's that. We make genuine sacrifice for those we will not see till heaven shall join us. For that reason I've planted 150 trees on this land, though I'll never see their fullness....For this reason I strive toward holiness, kindness and thrift." ("Of Seeds & Love & Legacies," p. 6)

And if we reverence the creation God has given to us to be stewards of, then when we need comforting, we can go to nature and be cradled in its comfort as we see God through his creation. "If I were out in the country now, I'd teach you the goodness of God's creation, even at night. I'd show you the stars and tell you their tales till they became your friends...I'd light the star of Bethlehem. I'd talk about angels, 'hosts of heaven' till the night skies were crowded with kindly spirits, and we were not lonely below them." (Little Lamb, Who Made Thee?)

"In the country I'd make you hear the wind; I'd teach you the breath of God, Spiritus Dei! God, who made it, keeps it all! The Creator laughs at the bullfrogs burp and loves the mockingbird - melodies, melodies, all night long. The phantom flight of the owl, the cricket's chirrups, the wolf's exquisite, killing, harmonies -- all these you would hear as the handiwork of God, just as you yourself are God's handiwork, and then you would be consoled." (Little Lamb, Who Made Thee?)

And if we learn to respect the creation of God we would be able to face death knowing that we are going from "creation to its Creator, to the God who conceived of Eden, and Paradise, and everything between the two. Better than the handiwork of God, dear heart, is God himself." ("When you Get There, Wait")

And if we listen to nature and are the caretakers of it as intended, we will see beneath the surface of the world and see "the entire story and myth behind the natural phenomena. Myth is convinced that Deity is greater than the world and can bring it to an end, but that Deity persists in writing legends in the clay of the world until the end shall come." (The Manger is Empty) And therefore, we need to see in nature its showing forth of the redemption of God:

"Therefore this Easter, I will go out and find the
    signs of Easter among these muter children
    of God.
I will apply to my brother forsythia. Bright and
    yellow, his light is my illumination: Christ
    has risen! The darkness has not overcome him!
I will touch the red drops of the dogwood and
    think of the wounds of Jesus.
I will marvel at the persistent return, the glad
    profusion of my sister jonquil and daffodil,
    whom dying cannot kill, but who will rise this year
    as any year before.
I will myself awaken in the waking of Creation, and
    I'll let its perfect obedience to all of God's laws be
    sermons unto me. And all its colors, all its variety, all
    its scents and sounds and forms shall instruct my tongue
    to praise with all my art the sweet Redeemer, liberator
    of all.

        Deo gratias!"

Shaping our lives with Words of Power

Chapter VI.

INVOLVING THE READER
THROUGH IMAGES

Shaping our lives with Words of Power

INVOLVING THE READER
THROUGH IMAGES

" Art is derived from the artist's power to conceive and bring forth images. These images are not an accumulation of parts; they are not a series -- they are a group of independent organs. But each image is a oneness - a totality. It is an intuition conceived and brought forth perfect. The artist conceives images complete, and (if he is a true artist) he conveys them to the reader complete....The real source of image is feeling; the image is but a symbol of feeling...mere factual knowledge is worse than nothing so far as art is concerned."

George C. Williams

Wangerin's unique power to develop images and through these images to involve the readers not only in the plot, character and surface of his works, but to engage them in the reality beyond his works is best seen in his longer fictional works. Here his images are developed fully, and their completeness and signifying powers are clearly seen.

Wangerin's images and symbols are strongly grounded in concrete descriptions, and they appeal to all of the reader's senses to create within the reader the emotions and experiences the author is attempting to convey. His details are not general but particular, interwoven, as in all of his works, with the themes of sin, evil, death, love, sacrifice, resurrection. These longer works appeal to the senses and don't convey factual knowledge to the reader but images, feelings, significance, and they invite the reader to enter completely into the cosmos of the work, evoking in the reader unique responses based upon the reader's own perceptions and background. Wangerin does not push morals, or tell the readers how to react to or interpret the works, but he allows the fictional work to evoke its own working on the individual. By his selection of details and their arrangement, and by his taking many familiar images and placing them in new connections and new environments, he renews the vigor and passion of the language, and readily enables the reader access to the deep feeling and significance of his novels.

Wangerin's narrations do not begin gently, but he forces the reader to face the world of the narrative from the very first sentence. Like the old storytellers of the oral tradition, the reader (hearer) has no opportunity to ease into the story. The initial parts of all of his longer works are specific in their opening details, and quickly create the cosmos the reader is to enter, and by subtly bringing in many elements of the conflict immediately, Wangerin begins in medias res (in the middle of the action) and instantly involves the reader.

Thus, Wangerin's first novel, The Book of the Dunn Cow, begins:

> "In the middle of the night somebody began to cry outside of Chauntecleer's Coop. If it had been but a few sprinkled tears with nothing more than a moan or two, Chauntecleer would probably not have minded. But this crying was more than a gentle moan. By each dark hour of the night it grew. It became a decided wail, and after that it became a definite howl. And howling, particularly at the door of his Coop, and in the middle of the night -- howling Chauntecleer minded very much."

Wangerin's foreshadowing in the words moan, dark hour, wail and his concrete descriptions all instantly involve the reader in the coming events of the novel. As Wangerin creates these images, the intensity of the setting, and the seriousness of the howling are further developed:

> "All the Coop had a healthy fear of awakening his feathered thunder. Therefore, when weeping became wailing, they pretended with a skill both admirable and desperate. And when wailing devel-

oped into pure howling, why, every last chicken turned into a stone.

'Marooned,' he cried, whoever he was out there. 'Marooned,' he wailed. Three stones sniffed and sixty eyes shot frightened glances at Chauntecleer, but the Rooster slept on...

And then he howled like the north wind: 'Maroooooooned!'

Chauntecleer stirred. He pulled one claw off the perch. Two chickens fainted...

'You,' said Chauntecleer in his sleep. Another chicken passed out.

...Chauntecleer was stunned. Seven chickens fainted dead away. But Chauntecleer didn't notice the bodies falling off their perches. He did something else."

As can be seen from the above passage, Wangerin's style is detailed and concrete, and he begins to bring forth the powerful images that will form the structure of the novel, and these images all appeal to the senses of the reader. Wangerin's language and choice of words are easily understood, and he has a simple surface which moves quickly, immediately engaging the reader in the story. As he composes this powerful novel, the internal complexity of the work and the underlying themes soon begin surfacing, and the reader is invited into the whole cosmos of Chauntecleer's universe. One soon forgets that these animals are not human, and they serve as perfect objective correlatives through whom the author achieves his emotional distance from the ideas and feelings he conveys, and yet is able to communicate these feelings and ideas to the reader evoking involvement in and openness to the work.

Although this novel and its sequel, The Book of Sorrows, are written in the 3rd person objective style, the narrator of the fables is so empathetically involved in the characters that there is no distance between the reader and the stories. The author's voice is exchanged in favor of the narrator's tale telling voice, and like all stories that are effectively told by a narrator, the hearer (reader) is drawn into the action. Wangerin's style throughout these two works is vivid with sometimes overly exaggerated images which enable the imagination of the reader to clearly " see" the story unfolding. For example, Mundo Cani's description of his nose:

> "And what about this nose?' cried the voice out-side...'All of you, count yourselves blessed. Go home and call yourself fortunate before the mirror! For if you wish, you can turn your eyes and look away from this monster of a nose. But me?
> '...I have to look at this nose all of the time, for here it sits between my eyes. Between my eyes, like a boot all the day long. Every time I look at anything, there is my nose underneath it. Ah me, me!...I am a walking sor-row. To look at me is to break your heart: but here is my nose, and I can look at nothing else but me. Marooned! Marooned in this sad excuse of a body!'"

Wangerin intermixes long and short sentences, and brings in abrupt interruptions of thought and repetitions of key phrases -- all keeping the pace of the story moving quickly and keeping the reader involved:

> "The earth had a face, then; smiling blue and green and gold and gentle; or frowning in furious gouts of black thunder. But is was a face, and that's where the animals lived on the surface of it. But under the surface, in its guts, the earth was a prison. Only one creature lived inside of the earth, then, because God had damned him there. He was the evil the ani-mals kept. His name was Wyrm....He lived in dark-ness, in dankness, in cold. He stank fearfully, because his outer skin was always rotting, a running putrefac-tion which made him itch, and which he tore away from himself by scraping his back against the granite teeth of the deep. He was lonely. He was powerful, because evil is powerful. He was angry."

The vividness of description, the repetition of images, and the intermingling of short and long sentences create a powerful style. The writing is " clear, concise, and bare." (Androski, p. 34) There is no ambiguity or unclearness behind which the reader can hide, and the story through its own internal consistency and precision of words draws the reader into itself. Wangerin brings in no detail that is not significant to the rest of the fable; he composes the images, foreshadowing the conflicts, hints at its resolution, and brings in no extraneous words or images. Each adds to the cumulative effect of the work. His images are whole and reflect Wangerin's accurate and minute observation of reality, and this careful observation enables the reader to see the world more clearly and to see more details than previously noticed. He repeats meaningful phrases and descriptions as a true storyteller does, piling one upon another to insure that the reader clearly envisions the setting.

Like all of his works, <u>The Book of the Dunn Cow</u> and <u>The Book of Sorrows</u> envision a universe where there is powerful evil and powerful good (the good may be ignorant of its strength and naive concerning evil, but its power is there). As <u>The Book of the Dunn Cow</u> begins, the known universe of the animals is orderly, a peaceful cosmos:

> "It encountered four seasons, endured night, rejoiced in the day, offered waking and sleeping; hurt, anger, love and peace to all of the creatures who dwelt upon it."

And Chauntecleer crowed canonical crows to sing the order of the universe to the animals:

> "These canonical crows...told all the world what time it was, and they blessed the moment in the ears of the hearer. By what blessing? By making these, and the moment of the day, familiar; by giving it direction and meaning and a proper soul...When Chauntecleer crowed his canonical crows, the day wore the right kind of clothes; his Hens lived and scratched in peace, happy with what was, and unafraid of what was to be; even wrong things were made right, and the grey things were explained."

But soon Wangerin foreshadows the coming conflict which will release evil and chaos into the world:

> "A third category of crows, within a year of Mundo Cani's coming to the Coop, burst from Chauntecleer's throat with a terrible power. For an enemy was gathering himself against the Rooster and this Land....This enemy hated God with an intense hatred...And what put the edge upon his hatred, what made it an everlasting acid inside of him, was the

knowledge that God had given the key to his prison in
this bottomless pit to a pack of chittering animals.

> Oh, it was a wonder that Chauntecleer the
> Rooster, that a flock of broody Hens, a Dog, a Weasel,
> and tons of thousands of suchlike animals -- should be
> keepers of Wyrm! The little against the large. The
> foolish set to protect all the universe against the wise."

And to add to the suspense and conflict, these animals are
unaware of the existence of evil and its power and of their role in
fighting it even though Wyrm cried all day: " Sum Wyrm, sub
Terra!" " Yet so deaf were the animals to the way of things that
even in this dreadful announcement they did not hear...Dumb
feathers made watch over Wyrm in chains! It was a wonder. But
that's the way it was because God had chosen it that way."

Thus, this beast fable, much like <u>Animal Farm</u>, enables the
reader to look wholly at the conflicts of life, identify with the
ignorance and blustering of the animals, laugh at their foolishness; but the parallels to the universe we live in are so accurately
and precisely drawn that soon the reader recognizes himself in
these animals and is drawn subtly into the overwhelming battle
between good and evil which forms the basis of this novel. At
first the conflict against evil is external -- the evil is named, visible, and the animals engage in battle. But as Wangerin does in all
his works, the reader soon realizes that the external, named evil,
is only one part, though painful. The stronger fight and the more
necessary one is the inner battle. As the narrator in <u>The Book of
the Dunn Cow</u> states:

> "Chauntecleer had won. Chauntecleer was victo-
> rious. But it is entirely possible to win against the
> enemy, it is possible even to kill the enemy, and still
> be defeated by the battle. Chauntecleer had not lost
> his life to Cockatrice, but he'd lost something infi-
> nitely more dear. He had lost hope, and with it went
> the Rooster's faith, and without faith he no longer had
> a sense of the Truth.
>
> ...Wyrm with seven words had struck down the
> leader of the land, so that the land was no longer
> proof against his escape. Leaderless, loose, the
> Keepers would lose their strength."

Wangerin in this seemingly simple beast fable adds layer upon layer to the significance of the events, and although the surface of the story is exciting, quick moving and entertaining, the reader is soon recognizing the depth of the tale, the power of evil, both inside and outside of oneself, and the absolute crucial nature of the battle being fought in this work -- a battle to keep chaos and evil from destroying the orderly world created by God; a battle to keep faith and hope alive inside oneself as one begins to recognize this evil and despairs at its strength; a battle to recognize love in others, to accept sacrifice, to understand that strength comes out of weakness. These themes developed in all of Wangerin's works reflect truthfully the universe in which we the readers live, and we are able to see the battles of life wholly through the power of this novel. We cannot gaze upon our own lives, but we " gaze upon these animals, which are symbols of our life and comprehends our own lives." And we begin to realize in " dreadful recognition that in these animals' characters there we are. We are lifted out of ourselves and enabled to see ourselves wholly." At this point of recognition, this fable of Chauntecleer " seems suddenly to reveal and make sense of our experience with the Deity. It becomes an archetype, a mirror, of our own drama; and rising to look carefully into it, we may thus look down upon the sublunary passages of our own faithing." And this experience enables us, within the cosmos of the novel, to recognize our own battles, and to gain courage to face the evil both within ourselves and without in the world.

Although the external battle against evil is intense and vividly described, it is the internal battle that becomes the focus of The Book of the Dunn Cow and The Book of Sorrows. Each of the characters is fighting despair, overcoming self-doubt, attempting to find courage and faith to fight the evil, and each is going through various stages of faithing and is interacting his drama with God. And Chauntecleer especially is attempting at the end of the battle with Cockatrice to recover his faith and to prove himself worthy of Pertelote's love and forgiveness and of God's. In order to overcome his doubts, he questions the evil in the world, the " whys" of the world, the silence of God. And like Pastor Orpheus in The Orphean Passages, there is no voice answering him:

"So Wyrm crawled the belly of the world. So.
But so what? He was still alive...and he took with him

a friend beloved above all others, that humble Mundo Cani.

> ...Mighty God, you talk to us! Tell us: Why does Wyrm exist?
>
> He killed peace.
>
> He killed their deeper trust and sweet security... Mighty God, please tell us. Explain it, explain -- Why is Wyrm?"

Chauntecleer, besides losing hope and faith during the war, realizes something else:

> "In his heart was the other question, and the nettle. The Rooster had lost another treasure to the war. Wyrm had killed self-confidence. That quality lay in him like a fetus dead and decomposing, and no one knew, none: Chauntecleer himself could hardly understand his heart's oppression. ...'Will you come (God), and will you tell me clearly, why? Why? Why does this Wyrm exist?'"

Wangerin's works are intense, scarcely giving interludes for the reader to relax and breathe before the characters are deeply involved in new battles against evil. Wangerin focuses in on the essential events of the character's lives, those signifying events, and enacts before the reader these events with a passionate voice. The only relief from the intensity is the pure moments of love and humor the characters experience as they attempt to make sense of the events of their lives and of the evil they have discovered in the world.

> "It is recorded with no surprise, that the Animals - even the children hatched after the war - lived grimly, chilly toward the world, spare regarding their own needs and of no particular hope in the future. Wyrm had murdered cheer. Cold realists were these Animals of the experienced eye....On the other hand, the tenderness toward one another grew intense -- how they loved each other, when suddenly the life in the other seemed so precarious, so rare, so precious."

The Book of Sorrows is a work which through the power of

the words in it evokes a cumulative effect of spiritual intensity. The depth of the spiritual probing by the author into evil, why it exists, the powerlessness of each of us in this struggle against evil, the seeming absence of God, our attempts at doing good on our own power, causing hurt instead of good, is purifying yet terrifying to the reader. The distance between these characters going through these sorrows and searchings and the reader who has recognized himself in the characters has nearly been collapsed so that the hurts become the reader's hurts, the questions, his questions, and the futile attempts at relieving the pain reflect the attempts in the reader's own life. And like Chauntecleer, all we can see as we cry out against evil is our own worthlessness:

> "And Chauntecleer, still without shifting his position, burst into tears. They were childish tears, great, wracking sobs and a total abandon to his sorrow. The dirt smeared in his beak and face. Oh, this was intolerable loneliness. Why had she come at all? Hadn't she known her holiness would torment him? ...Guilt is a knot, a thick lump in the gut, and a twisting pain. That's what the Rooster received...the knowledge of his guilt. It is a tumor worse than grief."

Wangerin uses all his artistic descriptive detail to ensure that the reader sees and feels the depth of the separation, guilt and despair each of us goes through on our faithing journey. He refuses to become sentimental and to fall back into religious clichés, but constantly, through meaningful repetition, adds image to image, trying to reach through the reader's mask of religious expectations. In this work and others, he begins with familiar religious concepts, juxtaposes them with strange and foreign backgrounds, startles the reader by the new images composed, in an attempt to find a new language through which the readers can truly hear the " old story" of God again. And in the majority of his writings, his attempts work -- they do clarify our visions, become mirrors in which we see our world better, and perform the functions of myths: they take us out of chaos, and enable us to create a cosmos out of it even in the midst of despair. Throughout most of Wangerin's works, chaos and evil almost triumph, and much of the power of the novels come from the near defeat of all that is good. And this is purposeful -- for an all-powerful evil, according to Wangerin, is needed to see an all-powerful good; death is needed to see resurrection; total helplessness, hopelessness and unworthiness is needed to see grace.

When we are going through despair, a sense of unworthiness, and a powerlessness in the struggle against evil, our world appears chaotic, the center no longer holds, and things fall apart. So in the world of Wangerin's novels, when Chauntecleer experiences despair, chaos begins to overtake the world:

> "Chauntecleer does not move. When he was done, he stood precisely where he was. But he was nowhere among his Animals, for his eye had hardened....That night no one came to sing Compline for the hens. No one came to touch his Pertelote. No, the darkness remained an alien depth, and the Animals did not sleep....In the morning Chauntecleer's lauds sounded like sleet, waking the hens with a miserable chilliness unlike the sunny praising they were used to...They bent to their work and thought: 'Why is he so angry with us?' The Canonical Crows had never been used for punishment before.

> And the Vespers Crow was a mere 'Quit.' And Compline dumped them to sleep - castaways.

> ...No longer did Chauntecleer interpret their moments and their experiences to them, nor did he recollect the past to weave it into the present, nor did he call them into a hopeful future; but that's what his Canon used to accomplish. He used to, by praising them or fussing at them, assure them of importance, and because he did it with such variety and skill...he was the glory in their homely lives...But lately the Canonical Crows had grown empty...Chauntecleer brooded and the world grew grey."

According to Wangerin, every culture needs its scop, its shaper, its poet or priest to weave the daily events into the eternal story of God. A society in which this shaping does not occur becomes crippled, one dimensional, and colorless. In each of his longer works, the main character goes through tremendous despair as he/she faces sin and evil, faces his own unworthiness, and no longer has hope, and, thus, can no longer give shape to the experience of life -- cannot make sense of the universe.

When Pastor Orpheus in <u>The Orphean Passages</u>, the eloquent

Pastor whose words preached life and meaning and significance into his parish's life, recognizes his worthlessness and despair, " he grew strange...His sermons became bookish things, preached from the pulpit and with notes. He'd never used notes before...God had turned away from Orpheus in disgust, as well he should...For Orpheus, God was not. Not because God was not powerful. Not because God was not good. God was good. God was good. Orpheus was not good."

Likewise in The Crying for a Vision, Fire Thunder recognizes that he cannot " offer a prayer for the dead. And because I could not do this thing, every other thing is dust....Old Woman, you are right. I have done no good thing in my life." And the power of despair of one person can cripple a whole people and the tribe passes through innocence to guilt and despair: " The Lacota did not dance in the Mystery Circle that year...The newly chosen itancan canceled the dance...Rather, they went on the warpath.

> "Whose spirit did this itancan worship?
> None.
> Whose rules did he obey?
> His own."

Sin, recognition of our helplessness, despair, loneliness, recognition of evil within and without one, are all necessary to the maturing character in Wangerin's work. And each character, when faced with the fact that he hurts others and has lost his hope, attempts to perform deeds to take control of life again to make himself worthy. As Chauntecleer despairs of the fact that he feared Wyrm, he decides to go down to the Netherworld by himself to kill Wyrm.

> " I will! I will!' Chauntecleer was crowing. 'I'll go that way to the Netherworld, and I myself will kill the evil one. And will set the good one free.'"

But Pertelote could scarcely breathe:

> "This was his (Chauntecleer's) something to do? Go down to Wyrm? Then he was going to leave her after all, and who did he think he was, that cock! That overweening cock! So self-centered in his moping and his guilt that no one, no one but himself could go face Wyrm! So blinding penitential that he could forget her!

> Chauntecleer had sworn an oath before heaven and
> all of the Animals...Now there was work to be done."

The work, the righteous deeds to be done, replace the emptiness and lack of faith and temporarily ease the loneliness and
pain. Or as Wangerin states in <u>The Orphean Passages</u>: After the
birth of our despair, " this is the passage of good works. This is
the period when the faithing one is convinced that his good works
also cause good consequences....Pastor Orpheus heard nothing
of...concerns regarding his health...This wasn't humility in him;
it was preoccupation. He was obsessed with his service. He was
seeking Jesus.

"Orpheus was seeking to be worthy of Jesus. He was, in fact,
seeking to breathe life into that carven figure of agony which
hung ever before his eyes. He wanted desperately to raise his
beloved Jesus from the dead; that is why he did all that he was
doing, and why he took the city to his heart. It was his mortification. It was discipleship, but solitary and unexplained."

As in real life, the rebirth of purpose and work in a leader or
Pastor causes many to see only the effectiveness of the service
and the unselfishness of the deeds, and the majority fail to see the
agony, loneliness and desperation beneath the surface, so in all of
Wangerin's novels, this stage of faithing creates great support for
the leader or character. The Lacota follow Fire Thunder to battle
after battle winning glory for him and for themselves: " they
began to dream a new dream, an exciting dream, one not even
considered by the people of the plains before....If they could then,
shouldn't they test the extremes of human achievement?...Fire
Thunder himself sat and said nothing. He watched
everything...and a thousand soldiers broke into song feeling very
happy." In the same way, Orpheus begins to preach more powerfully in the midst of his despair. " Orpheus, Orpheus! How do
you preach so well? You preach the pain of your heart's desire.
You preach your yearning...but though you entice an entire parish
to its feet by crying forth the name of Jesus, yet that passion
comes not of the presence of the Lord, but of his absence. It is a
beauty born of anguish." And Chauntecleer also inspires the animals: " And the Animals believed in him. They laughed. Their
eyes were stars, their voices full of worship, and their hearts
burst. They said: 'The spirit of God is upon him.' Then who could
resist his excitement?

"None, Neither two or two thousand...And Chauntecleer flushed with leadership."

But in the cosmos of Wangerin's fictions, any deeds performed in our own strength to prove our worthiness of God's love and forgiveness are doomed to be self-centered and hurtful to others, since they are ultimately based in arrogance and pride being products of a person's intensive desire to do something - to produce worthy deeds to deserve the love of others. Over and over in Wangerin's works, these deeds done in despair, even when they are " excellent" works of righteousness, produce intense hurt and even more suffering. Until the character learns to do nothing but wait on God and allow his forgiveness and love to comfort, he continues to destroy everything in the way of his good deeds.

So Chauntecleer cries out after wounding and killing so many: "'Oh no, we're not!' the Cock cries with sudden revulsion. 'I am nobody.'" ...and as Ferric tells him of the mercy of the beautiful, Gentle Dunn Cow, "Chauntecleer the Rooster delivers himself to grief. He is gulping the air and sobbing like an infant. His tears drill the dirty snow....So Ferric Coyote pulls his own poor body forward until he is next to the Rooster. Then he begins to lick Chauntecleer...and Chauntecleer burns.... 'Oh, God! Oh God!' howls Chauntecleer. 'Oh dear God, How can I stand this!' Every stroke of the Coyote's tongue wakens a wickedness in the Cock, draws it through his memory in order to wipe it away. It is a poor, pitiful life he remembers. No, this is no soft tongue...but the Rooster does not deny it, because it comes in kindness. Kindness is the reason it burns so much."

In the same manner, Orpheus realizes the hurts he has brought others through his righteousness. "How wrong the whole damnable world was!...this was the vile truth of his condition: he hurt people....Delores was righteous and gentle and kind and beautiful and undeserving of the pain he caused her....I am no Pastor. I am not worthy. Kindness hurts me."

Painfully, and in layered details, Wangerin describes the self awareness, and the final refinement to the " faithing one" in his novels -- death to the old self and death to all attempts at proving oneself worthy of others, of love, forgiveness and kindness. His works so perfectly mirror the Christian universe as he believes it to be that this death to our false selves, our attempts at control, and this final purging recognition of how even our righteousness hurts others when it is only done to hide the horrible despair inside and to prove ourselves worthy, permeates each novel. In each, this honest scene of self-recognition begins to bring resolution to the conflicts of the novels, for now the character is open to "hearing and seeing God" once again on God's terms instead of the character's terms. "First of all, the love of God is a terrible thing. It begins by revealing to us such treacheries and threats in the world that we know we must die soon." (Little Lamb Who Made Thee?)

And Wangerin graphically portrays this first love of God which brings about the death of our self and its efforts at self-control so that he can put this terrible love which so convicts us of sin, hurt, sorrow and unworthiness against the backdrop of the Resurrection and grace of God. According to Wangerin, God leads each of his children on these journeys to bring about the death of the self, so that he can truly create a new self in us. " God leads the faither unto himself not in a manner divorced from daily and worldly experience -- in the secret regions of the soul only -- but by means of the stuff and tumble of physical human existence. It is not a secret piercing of the heart that kills the faithing one, invisible to the eyes of other people. No, it is by the actions of these people themselves: it is in the very intercourse of community and words and feelings, bruisings, touchings, the casual greetings and the catastrophic attackings; it is in the downsetting and the uprising that God shapes the drama which kills the sinner. The spiritual drama of faith is enacted on the stage of this world, bodily and under sunlight." (The Orphean Passages)

So in each of his longer works, the realistic descriptions of all of the interactions of human beings -- the pains, the loves, the joys, the sorrows -- are all intertwined with his characters' dramas of faithing, and the hope and faith that is rekindled in each is intimately connected to every mundane detail of the novel. It has been those very details that have produced the spiritual changes in the main characters. The invisible workings of God are seen through the deep realism of the novels, and the endings of the works are direct consequences of the choices each character has made. But now, in Wangerin's works, when grace comes and forgiveness and salvation, it is as powerful as the evil and suffering that has preceded it. Powerful evil -- Powerful good -- These two are always brought together in his works -- the one always intimately connected with the other. No; his works, upon close reading, are not melancholic although they are filled with despair and

pain. They are realistic but always with a vision of hope - of forgiveness - of God and significance.

As he states:

> "Death shall come, dear God! The righteous execution
> of the sinner shall, by the gracious will of God, occur
> - and it shall most certainly have spiritual conse-
> quences; indeed, it is the spiritual interpretation of the
> event which names it 'death' at all. But it happens in
> the world and evidently. It takes place visibly before
> the eyes and by the actions of those who truly see, but
> do not understand what they are seeing....Death shall
> come. In what arena shall it occur? In the world's
> arena. By whose hand shall you be put to death? By
> the world's hand - though God shall turn that evil
> thing to good." (The Orphean Passages)

Wangerin continues to explain what this death is, and in each
of his longer works, this death is enacted before the reader:

> "What, exactly, shall this killing be? It shall be
> the stripping from you of any worthy identity in the
> world...You will be made to know yourself by the iso-
> lation and the pain inflicted...This surely shall be cru-
> cifixion.

> But it is at this point that the words 'I have been
> crucified with Christ; it is no longer I who live but
> Christ who lives in me,' tumble on the very edge of
> expression....It is now experience and no longer the
> inscrutable catechism of our youth, experience and no
> longer the Scriptural foundations of doctrine, experi-
> ence, our own Way, our vital Truth, and, since we are
> otherwise dead, our very life." (The Orphean Passages)

The forms of Wangerin's longer works vary so greatly - a
beast fable, the retelling of the Orphean myth, the reworking of
Lacota myths, personal experiences -- but all create a cosmos out
of the chaos experienced by the characters who are dying by the
" righteous killing of God." Each reflects the Christian universe
of love, mercy, sacrifice as it is almost lost and destroyed by the
un-naming and hatred of evil. And Wangerin's stories are " true"
in the sense that the Biblical stories are true for they see behind
the material realities and hurtful, self-centered actions to the wor-

ship of God. Although his main characters are flawed heroes, their stories are true, and each reader can recognize his/her faith journey in the works and cry: "There I am."

The despair, self-recognition, and final letting go of control, and thus dying, and the then accepting of grace and love are all stages necessary for the characters to undergo in order to be able to see the cosmos behind the chaos, the hope behind the despair. So Orpheus at the end is crying, not in despair but in joy: " 'Because I have seen the Lord,' he states...And Orpheus prayed. He prayed in perfect peace quietly, straight into the ear of Jesus. There were no distances any more between himself and his Lord, because this rental home was where Jesus lived, and it had been granted unto Orpheus to live there too -- the gift he had not asked because it was something he hadn't deserved." And at the end, Chauntecleer is being held by Pertelote, having accepted grace and forgiveness and his own guilt and he whispers: " 'The children were brave, dear Pertelote, because you are. Ah, my beautiful Pertelote. All these years, and all these happenings, and all your patience. Oh woman, I love you with all of my heart.'...And nobody wept. The time of weeping was over. They knew better, now. They knew to say <u>Is</u> and <u>Was</u> in righteous separation, to sit in the <u>Is</u>, to remember the <u>Was</u>, and themselves merely to be..." And when Pertelote sings, it is the voice of an angel singing order, harmony, and meaning into the world that had appeared so chaotic and meaningless. And in <u>The Crying for a Vision</u>, all the starvation and hurting and killing end, and the buffalo come back: " Tatanka was back. Our brother was home. The famine was over, and we could hunt again. Oh, there was so much work to be done. But first we had to give thanks: Pila miya Tunkashila! We danced in a sacred circle and we sang new songs and we cried in sorrow and we laughed in happiness because Wakan Tanka had decided to send us the red and blue days again."

And these endings are not carelessly attached to the work, they are a resolution to the conflict -- a resolution that rises directly from the realistic details and events of the works. They are the words of the storyteller giving shape to the amphorous and scattered events of daily life, weaving these events into the sacred story of God and signifying the events. Once the characters and the readers can see the strong arms of God holding them throughout the pain, sorrow, and death, they can literally " hover over boiling chaos and not be afraid" because the strength of the " story of God and of his involvement in the daily events has been revealed to them through the storyteller." Wangerin invites the readers to abide in his stories, to enter into them, and to bring the experiences and power of the story back to the mundane world of daily life so that it can be a lens through which we can see God's workings and a hearing aid by which we can hear God's still, small voice.

And his stories evoke strong responses from the reader - for they are artistically rendered, and the events are creatively selected to focus the reader and to affect the reader wholly: intellectually, emotionally and spiritually. Wangerin uses all of his intimate observation of the details of everyday life, refusing to omit even the smallest descriptive detail that might add to the imagery of his world. Anne Rives Siddons stated that "The writers I like most are either blessed or cursed -- as the case may be -- with a kind of third eye that can never close. As much as you would like to close that sucker and ignore details, you just can't do it." So Wangerin seems to be blessed (cursed) with a third eye that observes closely all aspects of reality, sees elements most people never see, and then reveals this seeing to the reader through his works. And his precision in language, his concrete descriptions, and his contextualizing everything into the events of daily life, keep the reader from being alienated from the works. The reader willingly accepts the world of his fiction, for the particular details employed by Wangerin decrease the distance between the narrator and the reader.

Wangerin's novels don't offer doctrines about life and about God, they offer relationships. "My stories are the meeting place in which relationships begin, mature, may be experienced whole, may be named, are certainly remembered, live." ("Telling Tales") "Religions have existed without theology...But no religion has existed without story...and the story is not story until it is told... Story does not instruct: Story makes a cosmos out of chaos. Because its form is itself an order, because it acknowledges and uses the elements of this existence as elements of itself, and because it invites the hearer into its world, it beds that hearer consolingly with all of his and her experiences, in an orderly and meaningful world. Story comforts....Doctrine may engage the understanding mind, but story engages the human whole -- body, senses, reason, emotion, memory, laughter, tears -- so the person who was fragmented is put back together again, and that under governance of a new experience - the hearing of his own story told....This sort of wholeness is not a truth to be believed and pre-served; it is itself experience." ("Telling Tales")

For the above reasons, Wangerin's longer works meticulous-ly and precisely create an orderly world so that the reader can have the courage to view the absurdity and chaos of life, and can feel the sorrow and destructive power of evil and yet can feel safe because he can also experience the meaningfulness and orderli-ness of God behind the chaos. Truth engulfs us in his stories sometimes in ways we don't anticipate, and God can break through our defenses and masks and "bushwack" us. Each of Wangerin's works are times of intense encounter with ourselves, with truth, with God, and yet each story becomes a discrete encounter for each individual reader. Wangerin states that he as a writer takes the "particular events of everyday life, the chaotic, often absurd events, and weaves them into the telling of the 'old, old story' until the center begins to hold again, and there is a world around the reader or listener once again." And because of the power of his words and of his stories to evoke emotional respons-es, Wangerin is careful to always tell " the truth of life and not to tell the reader a lie." "Our relationships with the divine can take a number of forms; some of these forms are healthier and more life-giving than others and some are oppressive and fear driven." (Sacred Stories, p. 25) Wangerin always attempts in his works to retell the organizing and life giving myths of our encounter with the divine and, in his longer fictional works, composes creative and constructive stories that reflect lasting truths. Wangerin, like Madelaine L'Engle, illuminates in his works that the purpose of any event is much more complex than it appears to the individuals involved in it, but the confidence that Wangerin holds is that behind those complex events is a pattern and behind that pattern is a loving God." "We are too small to see the richness of the whole, but all of creation is pattern." (Good, p. 191-192)

Through Wangerin's novels we can be lifted out of our small-ness, given the courage to virtually hover over the chaos of life, and from that perspective see the chaos and absurdity but also behind them the pattern and cosmos of life. Then as we leave the world of the novel which has comforted us with its visions of wholeness for a while, we can begin to discern the patterns in our own sorrowful and somewhat chaotic lives and, maybe, in the midst of the darkness see the patterns and hear the music of the spheres.

Chapter VII.

THE ORPHEAN PASSAGES

THE ORPHEAN PASSAGES

The work of Wangerin which most effectively demonstrates his belief in the power of words and his ability to speak with words of power is one of his earlier works, The Orphean Passages, 1986. Those who read this work agree that the work irresistibly draws the reader into it and into the path of discipleship, death, and resurrection of its main character, Orpheus. Forrester Church in his review states that "It is a poem of remarkable power...For me Lent began the day I finished this powerful book. Easter is further away than it has ever been, but I strongly sense the path to it more clearly than before." Or as John Timmerman states: "The cumulative effect of this tapestry carries a spiritual force that makes one wince with wonder."

Wangerin does not condescend to his reader in this work but forces the reader to think deeply, philosophically, and wholistically in order to comprehend the work. The beginning discussion of faith, change and language, and the theological discussion of each section are complemented by the story of the mythical Orpheus and Eurydice which is paralleled with the contemporary story of Pastor Orpheus. The stories of Pastor Orpheus, the myth of Orpheus and the theological reflections affect the reader as a whole person and demand a thorough insightful reading not just a surface glossing for events and plot. Thus, many readers who have picked up the work expecting to be entertained soon become discouraged by the beginning discussions on language and faith, and many never get past the Introduction and the First Passage. But for the person who desires to mature in his/her faith and to comprehensively feel the power of the death and resurrection of Christ and of the individual following Christ, this work is probably one of the most powerful and mature written during the last many years. As Wangerin states in his introduction concerning his work: "It is absolutely necessary if I am to say that faith is experiential also to show it so -- and by my art to trigger experience for the reader. Please, all the weapons of my art are used."

Wangerin uses all of the myths of Christianity about the human condition of sin and bewilderment and of death and redemption, and through the character of Orpheus these truths of the Christian faith become experiential rather than intellectual only. This work, more than any of Wangerin's others (except for The Crying for a Vision) communicates in a mythical whole and brings to the foreground for the reader all the primary concerns of humans: meaning and significance, love, acceptance, death of self, resurrection, love of God and forgiveness. Wangerin's work gives to the reader an understanding of the depth and breadth his response to God must embrace if it is to be a realistic response, one that has faced the negative powers of the world. As he states near the end of the Fifth Passage: "It is now that the experience which he (St. Paul) declares has become our experience...experience and no longer the inscrutable catechism of our youth, experience and no longer the Scriptural foundations of doctrine, experience, our own Way, our vital Truth, and...our very life...'I have been crucified with Christ, nevertheless I live, yet not I but Christ lives in me...Not as shades, but as flesh and blood we experience the resurrection (both here and hereafter)...No, we do not follow cleverly devised myths when we made known to you the power and the coming of our Lord Jesus Christ, but we are eyewitnesses of his majesty and love.'"

"The sort of knowledge gained (from The Orphean Passages) is the subtle education of our 'situation conscience'; it is what happens to our sensibilities when we are still and absorb the complexities and intricacies of the human spirit and the depth and subtleties of evil...the sort of knowledge gained (from the work) is not in terms of programs, rules or gimmicks that tell us what to do or think; it is an insight into man's being that influences our attitudes toward our fellows and our awareness of the humans' situation in the world that forces our Yes to God's rule to come from the heart and not from off the top of our heads." (Sarah TeSelle)

And this experience gained from this work, for the reader who has carefully absorbed the beauty and complexity of

Wangerin's work, becomes a lens through which one can see more clearly and experience more fully the truth of the Christian faith. And although the internal complexity of the work makes it difficult, the "felt experience" received makes the novel well worth the energy one puts into it. In fact, this work is one which needs to be read slowly and meditatively, for its emotional intensity and expressed truths can overwhelm the reader.

Wangerin begins <u>The Orphean Passages</u> with a long discussion of language, faith, and change. As is usual with this author, he does not easily seduce the reader into his work, but plunges him immediately into a deep philosophical discussion, and this first section can immediately alienate the casual reader. His first sentence sets the tone: "We desire our nouns to declare the fixedness of things...We 'noun' our verbs, as it were. We do that to comfort ourselves; we identify and codify natural laws to comfort ourselves; laws are the nouning of our terrible verbs." Then he comes home closer to the reader..."Likewise precisely, faith is 'faith' not in the building it, but only in the fixed condition -- or so we desire. Faith ought never to change. We desire the noun faith to declare a fixed position, especially when the rest of existence so bewilders us. Let faith noun one thing absolutely. Faith is, in our wish and in Shakespeare's words, 'an ever-fixed mark, that looks on tempests and is never shaken.' Everything flows? Maybe.

"But not faith! So plead our souls. Not faith, the God in us and we in him. No, not faith -- or nothing at all is left."

But the changings in our relationship to God are what this work wishes to make experiential to the reader, so Wangerin refuses to give the comfort of faith as a non-changing noun to the reader, and prefers to show the "truth" of faith even though to do so requires the death of many Christians' favorite clichés and catechistic beliefs. And since Wangerin perceives faith as an ever changing relationship or drama with the Deity it does "not subsist in definitions which freeze it to objectify it, but is the changing itself. The changing is the livelihood of relationship...Faith is relationship. But relationship dies in doctrines about it; at least it hides the while...Faith is personal and must be faithing...When we believe in faith's fixedness, then we have come to believe in words, in the nouns and the commission of our nouns -- in doctrines, but not in God....Faith flows. To be in faith is ever to be changing...To be in faith is ever to be moving through the passages of faith and to be moved by them. It must be a verb, then: faithing."

This discussion is absolutely necessary to the completeness of The Orphean Passages, for it shatters any illusions that the reader may have that this is going to be another typical, shallow, clichéish Christian novel. And the reader, who reads meditatively through this first section, is prepared for the story which is to follow. Wangerin has been criticized by some for the opaqueness and difficulty of this introduction and first chapter: "Sadly, many readers will never get to the final three-quarters of the book. Wangerin's prologue, and extended essay on the meaning of language and the language of meaning is almost unintelligible, far more precious than profound, and filled with jargon (he talks of 'faithing' and 'nouning' and how this 'faither' has to 'verb it.' Making entry into this book is even more difficult in the fact that the first chapter, which recounts the Rev. Orpheus' childhood, is riddled with theological pretensions." (Forrester Church)

But Church and others miss the power and depth and necessary preparation for the reader of these first sections. They are not added, inconsequential or irrelevant -- they are basic to the total impact of the work. Many readers need to be shocked out of their easy, fixed definitions of being in and out of the faith, and they need to realize how limited our experiences can be by the language we employ to describe them - only then can we be ready for the stages of change and the drama that follows along with the death of the old self and the rebirth of the new self.

Wangerin creates no new theological concepts or ideas in this book, but the way he composes the events and organizes the Christian's drama with God in various dynamic stages makes the reader understand and feel the depth of this drama and relationship with God (maybe for the first time.) Wangerin doesn't weaken the impact of our self-centeredness, our constant hurting of others (even our righteousness), our fears, our doubts, and eventual death of self - in fact, he makes the experience of these elements almost too unadorned and too harsh. The reader wonders if he/she can handle the emotional impact of recognizing oneself in the character of Pastor Orpheus and in the classical myth of Orpheus for, if these two intertwining stories work as Wangerin intends for them to, they become a symbol, "Shorn and unadorned, refined and true. And when the one who gazes upon that myth suddenly in dreadful recognition cries out, 'There I am! That is me!' then...he is lifted out of himself to see himself wholly... This particular myth (of Orpheus) teaches us the heart suffering of faith." Wangerin's contemporary Orpheus, Pastor Orpheus, is one moving through the passages of faith, and as he experiences his relationship with God, all aspects of this drama are fully revealed - his sins, conscious and unconscious, his pride, his love, his hurt that he causes others, his death to self and death to God and his final Resurrection, and "As Orpheus does, so do we enact a drama with our God...He is not always to be trusted, but his story is."

The reader is now prepared to allow Wangerin to work his art and to weave his story with words of power, so Wangerin begins his telling of the myth of Orpheus in six passages interweaving the parallel passages in the contemporary Orpheus and reinforcing these passages with heartfelt theological discussions which enable the reader to intellectually understand the deep experiences of these two stories.

The first passage begins with Orpheus' beautiful, potent singing and his love of and marriage to Eurydice, and our Pastor Orpheus begins to learn the power of words to name his encounter with and love for the divinity. And all children, and each of us as readers, begin our faithing experience as children, but it can according to Wangerin, "in the vast massacre of neglect, die." But some children do receive a language to speak their experiences with God and "some are trained in it by a community who trusts in its truth." Orpheus was one of those who learned a language. And in this first passage Wangerin parallels the two stories:

> "Orpheus loved Eurydice long in the mists of our unmemory; but then, once, publicly, he spake his love in a vow, and they were married. That was a holy moment.

> "Thirteen-year old Orpheus loved Jesus long...even in the mists of his own unremembering; he loved him deeply...and then he, too, named his love in a vow and publicly married himself unto his Jesus. His love rose into view. And the moment was very, very holy."

This confession of Jesus is the first stage in the faithing journey, according to Wangerin. But, as he states at the end of the first passage: "Many of those confessors stop, right here where they are. They presume that this confession, this clear commitment ('I have accepted Jesus in my heart; I am saved!') is the full accomplishment of faith. They have arrived....All that is left, they believe, is to go forth boldly with the Gospel, themselves examples of -- and witnesses to -- its finished product, since for them the heavenly marriage is fixed. For them the fluidity of a living relationship has been boxed in doctrine; dialogue has hardened into liturgy (or hymns repeated, or repeated prayers), and the creating word would horrify them, could they hear it. Their words from the Creator are laminated in the pages of their Bibles, unchanged, unchanging, unalterable forever." "And when they watch what happens to Orpheus hereafter, they do not understand."

Thus, Wangerin with elaborate words, philosophical interchanging of ideas, and long, involved sentence structures begins his novel where most religious novels end - the conversion of the Christian. But for Wangerin, this is only the first stage of the faithing journey, necessary lest we lose our belief in angels and God along with our belief in Santa Claus, but a child's first step, nevertheless. As he states at the end of the First Passage: "But for Orpheus, faith is faithing.

"It began in love and a marriage...But time does not stand still...It moves. Faith leads, if it doesn't deviate its proper course, to pain and unspeakable pain...

"Grieve for the grey-eyed Orpheus. He will move through hell to that passage where...language shall stun him, finally, with a name -- and with being."

This work by Wangerin would be valuable reading if only for this retelling of the Myth of Orpheus, for he makes this story, unknown or un-understood by so many modern people, come to life, and this character of Orpheus becomes full bodied and dynamic. And as he passes through the next stages so does our contemporary Orpheus -- first the naming of his love, then death and mourning (the death of Eurydice and the death of the experience of Orpheus' Lord.) This second passage is vividly described by Wangerin; when the death occurs, we "qualify the horror of the thing. We say, 'I just don't feel it any more.' We blame, perhaps our own weak faith or backsliding, our failure to keep faith, to pray as we should, to study....There comes to the Faithers the Easter without joy. There comes the Gospel without substance. There comes that morning when the Son and the sun don't rise again."

Only a writer who is desperately honest about his journey with Christ and who himself has acknowledged those intense and grievous moments when God seems absent and the world seems empty could write this section. And as Wangerin states: "This death is not uncommon...The faither still believes, and she still loves Jesus. Or she would love Jesus, if she could find the warm Lord to be the receiver of that love. But she can't. So all these things grow cold and stony and more hollow than the tomb of Joseph of Arimathea. There comes the gospel without life." And what happens in this second stage? "The faither becomes angry; hymns and rituals of the faith make one impatient. The traditions of the church become suffocating...And the terrible void remains...To despair: That is the third face of grief, when the mourning has arisen...And yet all these convulsions of grief are a passage within the drama of faithing, very much a part of faith and not apart from it...This is faith. This is faithing."

Wangerin at this point in his telling of the faithing journey echoes many thoughts expressed by Hermann Hesse in his description of the faithing experience. According to Hesse, faith begins in childlike innocence and love, then if it is to become genuine, passes into the second stage of despair, awareness of sin, and the dark night of the soul. But like Wangerin, Hesse doesn't leave the faither here -- he states that we then become overwhelmed by our sense of sin both in the world and in ourselves and attempt to retreat into good works or denial before we go further in our journey. Likewise Wangerin leads the faither through mortification and supplication. As Orpheus descends into the underworld and sings to find his Eurydice, so Pastor Orpheus descends into the inner city and sings of his faith, unaware of others praising his works for he is too intent upon his labors. And as Orpheus' descent to the underworld brings to him the "ceaseless groanings of those who have been falsely accused...and the shocked cries of the suicides...and the shrieks of usurers...Orpheus is not "deaf to the outrageous enormity: This is what humanity can do...To enter hell is to learn that Hell has entered life above and is the darkness not only under the earth, but in the human heart. No one chooses such knowledge -- except Orpheus alone, because he loved." So the Pastor Orpheus sees the "depth of the sinful suffering of the city. There is a darkness there; and in that darkness people wail their sorrows in a thousand minor keys. It is a strident hell of noise...Into that darkness, down into that gloom of confusion, Orpheus chose willingly to descend -- to serve...Orpheus was obsessed with his service. He was seeking Jesus."

But at the end of this descent into Hell we get a glimpse of Jesus, just as Orpheus gets a glimpse of Eurydice -- but "the vision of Jesus (and Eurydice) and its vanishing happen at once." But this descent and this brief glimpse of Jesus is only another necessary part of our faithing journey, for the "fourth passage of faithing is darkness."

Once again Wangerin goes to the myth of Orpheus to help the reader understand and experience this fourth stage of darkness. And Orpheus is allowed to bring Eurydice back to the living world if "he would always look forward -- never look back to see if Eurydice was following him." He needed "to trust her attentions, knowing nothing....It meant not seeing at all the very purpose for which he labored. Trust."

So the Christian is asked to trust God and to go in the gladness and the memory of our sweet experience of Jesus....So what do we have as time passes and the memory of our experience with Christ fades? The darkness in which doubt occurs. And doubt becomes a question: And what do we have? The silence which absolutely refuses to answer that question. So the question recurs again and again to hector us:

Jesus? Are you there?

Silence.

Jesus.

"A silence so deep that it doesn't even whisper: Trust. How bad can it be? As bad as to battle the devil. That bad. That hazardous. As bad as battling every tendency within yourself...."

But as Wangerin explains, faithing in the fourth passage calls for the sacrifice of our independent selves and our willful action, and also of the patterns whereby we live and apprehend the truth. So into this passage of darkness, Pastor Orpheus descends; and now that Wangerin has prepared the reader by the myth of Orpheus and by his explanations and illustrations, the reader is led with Orpheus into the darkness of finding out that his parishioners loved him not Jesus, that there is only silence as he begs: "Jesus, are you there?...And in time there appeared a certain haunted expression in the Pastor's eyes...And this is what was happening in the ministry of Pastor Orpheus...No one seemed to be changing for the better. The distress grew sharper in him, and the darkness intolerable..." and "the silence of God was killing."

But this necessary passage, according to Wangerin, plunges us even deeper into our awareness of sin and idolatry and like Peter, when he denies his Christ, so we too, have sinned and the next glance of Christ is caused by our sin. "It is not our love, but our sin that called him up...We denied his very nature! We commanded him to be dependent on visible signs...By our doubt, our mistrust, we had all along been seeking to exchange the hidden glory of the immortal God for images resembling mortal humanity...With Peter, we go out to the narrow street between two walls, the wall of the culpable past, the wall of the hopeless future, and weep bitterly."

Wangerin by his masterful intertwining of the myth of Orpheus, the stories of Pastor Orpheus in the inner city, the Biblical stories which symbolize these same passages of faithing and his clear commentary, has affected the reader powerfully in all ways: emotionally, intellectually, spiritually, even subconsciously, and the symbols employed create responses too deep for explanation. But unless the reader has been willing to leave his childish, secure, unquestioning faith, and has truly allowed "faithing" to occur, Wangerin's novel at this point could almost seem melodramatic, for the emotions of the Pastor Orpheus are extreme -- but extreme only in their attempt to portray in words an inward struggle that has deep roots in the soul of each believer.

But Wangerin believes that only the person who has truly experienced the death and loss of Christ, and the death of false idols and of the false self which follows, can truly experience the grace and wholeness of the resurrection of self and of Christ. And all of his works are attempts to get the reader to get rid of misconceptions and the false self so that the truth of Christ's love and forgiveness can be experienced. Thus these four passages of faithing are necessary to the faithing one if he/she is to once again (or for the first time) truly experience the resurrection. This stage of darkness, according to Wangerin, ends in guilt and despair, and leads the faithing one into the final sense of sin, separation, and dying. So Orpheus as he loses Eurydice because he glanced behind him, faces the final sense of sin, separation, and dying, so Pastor Orpheus faces the final rejection of himself and his own death -- he loses the respect of his church members, his pastoral position, and his death (death of his old need to do good, ask for signs, justify himself.) And Pastor Orpheus sees that "'This is who I am now. This is what I do. I hurt people.' He despised himself. He despaired."

But as Wangerin carefully explains to the reader, this death is necessary and is a good thing in the life of faithing:

> "Death shall come, dear God! The righteous exe-
> cution of the sinner shall, by the gracious will of God
> occur -- and it shall most certainly have spiritual con-
> sequences; indeed, it is the spiritual interpretation of
> the event which names it a 'death' at all. But it hap-
> pens in the world and evidently...This surely shall be
> crucifixion..."

But as Wangerin continues his faithing journey, he does not leave the reader in despair for this death, the realistic appraisal of one's inability to do anything, for all these events and realizations contribute to one's ultimately experiencing Christ truly rather than merely intellectually knowing him, and all are necessary to our being born as new creatures in him and understanding the depth of the mercy of God and the power of his resurrection. And Wangerin's works never leave the reader in absurdity, despair, and death but always with hope, significance and resurrection.

As he states in the final passage of faith - we are creatures of a Creator. He is the teller of this tale, telling it not in the spheres of the imagination but in this world, in space and time, in fact. We do experience his telling it. We end alive, becoming...what the Greeks but dreamed of, what God does give. Not as shades, but as flesh and blood we experience the resurrection (both here and hereafter)...For at this point in our drama with God, we, like Pastor Orpheus, experience the Resurrection and the Life, the Lord himself - not acknowledge him but experience him. Wangerin is totally honest regarding the doubts, sins, and self-centeredness of his character because he believes that "behind the events is a pattern and that behind that pattern is a loving God."

Like Madelaine L'Engle, Wangerin uses the power of the Biblical stories and of the Greek myths, and he believes that these myths are "true" and show the patterns behind our daily actions - even the seemingly irrational daily events. "There is a violent kind of truth, a timely truth, in the most primitive myths because probably the most important thing these first storytellers did for their listeners was to affirm that the gods are not irrational, that there is structure and meaning to the universe....Truth happens in these myths. That is why they have lasted. Had they not been expressions of truth, they would have long ago been forgotten....The books in the Bible that have stayed with us are those that are true, that speak to us in our daily living, right where we are now." (L'Engle, "Before Babel") So Wangerin in this work reveals the patterns behind the chaos of Pastor Orpheus' life by relating the individual events in his life to the great truths of the Greek myth, and to the stories of the Biblical scriptures - He becomes the "scop" who retells the daily events, finds the patterns in them, and helps the reader make sense of the chaotic and seemingly random events in his/her life. Then our faith, as his readers, becomes experiential like the faith of Pastor Orpheus. "Now we know it well enough to say it: we know it by experience...and though, between our sense of his crucifixion and our experience of our own, there seems to be a pitiful number of false stops and folly, yet it was all embraced by faithing, and in that sense it was right. No, not that we were righteous, but rather than righteousness was served by all of it, even by our pride and the manifestation of our sinfulness. In the broken world, given the character we bring into the drama, it had to be....No, we do not follow cleverly devised myths when we make known to you the power and caring of our Lord Jesus Christ, but we are eyewitnesses of his majesty and love..."

Wangerin collapses time in this work so that the Orphean myth, the Biblical stories, Pastor Orpheus' childhood and adulthood and our experiences of these are all occurring in Kairos (God's time) and are, thus, contemporaneous to one another. When Orpheus loses Eurydice, we are there with him; when Pastor Orpheus fears for his Mother or is in darkness and despair, we are there; when Mary Magdelene is crying at the tomb of Jesus, we are there. Since we usually are looking back on events (such as Christ's death, and know the end of these events,) this collapsing of time enables us to experience the horror of the loss in each of these examples as if we were truly experiencing them, and this experience enables us to understand the significance of Christ's death and our death, his resurrection and our resurrection, rather than just to understand them in doctrines and words. Like Dilsey in William Faulkner's The Sound and the Fury: "We have seen the beginning and we have seen the end, and now it all makes sense." So this work enables us to truly see the beginning (death, sin) and to truly see the end (forgiveness, resurrection), so now the events and sufferings of this life make sense.

As we journey with Pastor Orpheus through his sorrows and death, his recognition of his sin and his attempts at self-healing, we recognize this same journey in ourselves are we are desperate for the mercy of God -- not a theological knowledge of it or a doctrine about it, but the experience of God's mercy, of God's angels speaking to us. So the laughter of Orpheus' Mother, the laughter of the author and of us as we watch Mary still unaware of the Resurrection, and the laughter of Tulip as Orpheus prays in perfect peace gently straight into the ear of Jesus -- all these enable us to experience the joy of mercy, forgiveness and resurrection. And as Arabelle clutches her stomach because the new life in her is about to be born, so we all clutch our stomachs and experience our own birth pangs as we have traveled with Orpheus through suffering, death, Hell, love, forgiveness and resurrection. As Eugene O'Neil had Lazarus laughing when he comes out of the tomb because of Christ's calling his name, so we hear Christ call us to a new life by calling our name just as he used Mary Magdelene's name to birth her:

> "As God spoke all creation in the first place, so it was his word that woke you...
> But the word was you. You were freed by it.
> One word! He chose no other word by which to raise you from the dead, by which to work one wonder and a thousand, than your own name...
> He said, 'Mary!'
> The shepherd called his sheep by name, and the sheep became a sheep, knowing his voice and knowing that she was known by him. How did it feel?
> The Lord said 'Light,' and there was light:
> The Lord said, 'Mary,' and there was Mary...
> He said 'Mary,' and you, stapheisa, turned. He named you. He raised you, that you might announce his resurrection to the world."

The Orphean Passages is full of symbols, images, complexity, yet tightly structured so that all the various events from Greek culture, Biblical culture, contemporary culture, theology join together to enable the reader not only to grasp but to experience the truth of the Christian faith. The storyline captivates the reader's interest, the beauty of the language in the retelling of familiar myths and stories makes the reader delight in the sound of the work, and the depth of the theology explained and "storied" and the truth brought forth, all are Wangerin's unique writing talents at their best. One does "wince with wonder" at old truths so often explained, but so seldom experienced.

Chapter VIII.

THE CRYING FOR A VISION

Shaping our lives with Words of Power

THE CRYING FOR A VISION

"The boy felt sorry for his sin a long time. And now he has confessed it. This is important since only the unconfessed and unforgiven sin destroys things, Waskn Mani...So he said, 'What if the sin is not confessed? What if it is not forgiven? What then?'

The wolf, fixing him still with her steadfast eye, said: 'When the sin is great it breaks the circle of the world and when the hoop is broken, everything suffers. Everything.'

The word she used for 'circle' was hocoka, the same one by which the Lacota refer to the circle of tipis in the village. Were village and the world the same too? Could this be?

The boy said, 'What do you mean, The Circle of the world?'

'Waskn Mani, every creature is appointed to serve another. That's hocoka, the sacred hoop. If someone for selfishness ceases to serve, the circle breaks and creatures go hungry. The more who hunger, the fewer there are to serve until everyone suffers. When everyone suffers the world itself may die. That's what happens when a sin is not forgiven.'"

With these few words Wangerin develops one of the important symbols of his tightly written, deeply symbolic story <u>The Crying for a Vision</u>. Although he uses the Indian legends and mythology of the Lacota people throughout the work, the world presented intimately reflects the Christian vision of the world: sin, self-centeredness, evil, death, suffering, sacrifice, forgiveness, love, new life, hope. "This work," according to Wangerin, "produced after many years of studying this culture, presents the Lacota as that common people in whom all might see themselves...For I have found in the Lacota vision a rich analogue for the relationship any people of genuine faith experiences with creation and the Creator....Reader...Look not at the tale but through it for the truth."

This meticulously written and well structured work uses the Lacota people and their legends as the objective correlative through which the author can achieve emotional objectivity without losing the reader's emotional involvement in the work. Structured much like the stories of oral tradition, the narrator involves the reader in the action and adds detail upon detail until the reader "sees" the images and comprehends with his senses the physical world of the Lacota and understands the deeper truths of their legends and myths.

Like most stories in the oral tradition, the story starts in the middle of the story, causing the reader to wonder why and what the significance of the events are. "Now then, the story starts here, with a small question: why was a five-year-old child sitting in the tipi of the chief, a little boy cross-legged and scowling as fierce as the rabbit? What could have been the reason for this boy's elevation?" From this point, the surface of the story moves quickly and simply, but the internal complexity becomes apparent as the boy's past, his mother's childhood and death, and the other events are told by the narrator through a series of conversations, flashbacks and revelations.

Within the first few pages of this work all of the major conflicts are hinted at, all the major characters introduced, and the reader realizes that something much deeper than a simple story of an ordinary five-year-old Indian Boy is about to occur.

"'This is your trouble,' he whispered.

'Not his success,' Slow Buffalo said, 'But his manner. There is something here that scares me concerning our future.'"

So Fire Thunder is introduced by Wangerin, and this warning

from Slow Buffalo dominates the reader's first meeting of Fire Thunder. "Oh, what a man now unfolded beside small Waskn Mani: as for height more glorious than the timberland, a man like a single cottonwood standing alone midfield, tall and tough...The right eye flashed like black obsidian: the left remained as mysterious as God...He fights in silence, the young men said. He fights in solitude. He never cries out and even when he is done, he does not utter stories. Others must sing his glories for him." Thus, the narrator brings the two major characters together, the one small and powerless - the other huge, stonelike and alone. And the conflict between the two becomes apparent even at the beginning for as he sees the boy "his reaction was so strange that Waskn Mani, seeing it, didn't speak again."

> "Fire Thunder first had narrowed his eye at the five-year-old but now he opened it in seeming recognition and his face seemed to swell with emotion. His visible eye ignited with fire, his brow grew black, he lifted his right hand and pointed at the boy as if to say, 'Don't speak to me, Don't speak to me, boy!' In fact, the man said nothing at all, but a hissing escaped his teeth.

> Without a word...without prayer or approval or an end to the ritual, the warrior stood, bent down and departed the tipi. He went forth like an owl in perfect silence."

Wangerin masterfully integrates all of the Lacota symbols in this work, using them as integral to the forward moving action, but also allowing them the power of symbols to point beyond the narrative surface to deeper truth. "The Lacota value symbols highly," according to Julien Rice, "not simply for what they point to, but as a means by which the soul grows and changes." ("Symbols: Meat for the Soul") And the importance of carefully reading symbols is emphasized in the characters of this work. As the child Waskn Mani is mourning and feeling "very sorry for the weeping star," Slow Buffalo, itancan of the band, gives him some advice:

> "Slow Buffalo said, 'Wachin ksapa yo. That is my advice.' Now he did not look up, directly into the young boy's eyes. He said, 'Be attentive, boy. Pay attention to every being because anything might be

carrying the news of heaven down to you. Anything. Do you hear me?'

Solemnly Waskn Mani nodded.

'Wachin ksapa yo. Be attentive. Even an ant can tell the truth, but who would know this if first he does not listen to the ant?'"

Wangerin carefully reveals through this fictional work the importance of listening and hearing the message in each symbol for the listener, importance not only to the listener but to his people and to the earth. Julian Rice confirms this importance: "The importance of carefully reading symbols is emphasized in the Lacotas....One of the most important requisites for a wise person ...is the ability to read symbols. Any animal, even an ant, may speak to a person. The speaking implies receptivity to a divine message through any of his creations. It also implies that all living things are one, and are constantly expressing that unity to him who has been emptied of a noisy self....Reading attentively, in order to discover one's identity as a spiritual being...frequently involves freeing the self from fears of social ostracism." ("Symbols: Meat for the Soul")

Thus the journey of the orphan, Waskn Mani, is to find his own unique spiritual self. Although an orphan and an outcast from the people, he goes against the people and learns to listen to all creation. Yet, he feels "frightened and alone," and incurs the wrath of Fire Thunder, who is so filled with himself that he cannot read any symbols spiritually and opposes the young boy's quest. Yet Waskn Mani is able to "see holiness in everything, everything laid the great weight of holiness upon his soul...and the boy feels so ashamed of his people. He feels sorry for the star...and he feels so lonely. Only Standing Hollow Horn, Waskn Mani's Grandmother, and Slow Buffalo, the three older members of the Lacota people, are able to perceive the specialness of this young man and to see through the overpowering Fire Thunder and the materialistic, destructive power of his "non-spiritual" visions. Fire Thunder destroys all of the symbols and myths of the people causing great blood shedding, famine and destruction while Waskn Mani suffers deeply, listens to the smallest of God's creatures and causes great love, sacrifice and ultimate healing. But these two powerful forces are opposed throughout the fictional work until evil is widespread, and there is much death, destruction and famine, and the land and its people are dying. All the living creatures have also left the land, and the center of the sacred circle is broken.

As Fire Thunder is being elected itancan of the Lacota people, Waskn Mani cries out: "Fire Thunder murdered my Mother. Fire Thunder killed as well the mothers of these children here. There was no reason for the slaughter. He did not ask. In the evil of his heart he slew them! He shot them with arrows, and those he could not shoot he burned. No, Lacota! No, No, this man must not be an itancan of my people -- or else the nation will become sick with his sin."

As he states this, Fire Thunder comes out of the Eastern darkness...and chaos "had come to both sides, one side scrambling and stampeding to escape death, the other rushing to battle and to kill....There was one more song that sorry night, a lamentation deep and terrible. Some said the animals sang it. This is certainly possible. Others, however, said the singing came from the sky, that the stars themselves were mourning. Waskn Mani's grandmother said: 'No, It is the earth. Maka is weeping for her children.'"

Because of Fire Thunder's evil heart, his rejection of all things sacred, and his self-filled leading of the Lacota, chaos is unleashed on the earth, the sacred circles are broken, and the center of the Lacota universe no longer holds.

"It is no small thing to record that the Lacota did not dance in the Mystery Circle that year.

They dropped the Sacred Cottonwood. It touched unconsecrated ground. This was a desecration, but it was not irredeemable.

Nevertheless, the newly chosen Itancan canceled the dance. The Holy Men of every band disputed the decision. Was there ever a year where a people had not danced?

Never. For how could a nation prosper if it had not honored Wakan Tanka or humbled itself before him in prayer and sacrifice. Well, it could not. But this chief was impenetrable...

Whose Spirit did this Itancan worship?
None.

Whose rules did he obey?
His own."

Thus in Wangerin's work, a whole people is brought sorrow and death by one human, and the events of the following two years are bloody, fearful, and end in famine as all of the animals desert the land.

With great skill Wangerin interweaves all of the sacred circles, all of the destruction, the isolation of Waskn Mani and his grandmother, and the fears and sorrows of the people as death, violence and loss of myth and purpose occur to the Lacota people. The narrator moves forward quickly as the paths of Fire Thunder and Waskn Mani diverge for two years - the one following his spiritual quest through loneliness and sorrow until he learns sacrificial love, the other following his own spirit and his own rules until the entire nation suffers death, despair and barrenness. As Waskn Mani's grandmother holds him in his sorrow and sings the old song to him, Fire Thunder leads his hot-blooded warriors in "war parties as huge as storm clouds conquering and to conquer." Soon, however, the Lacota begin to notice the change in the earth itself... "By the end of the summer the women were wondering where the buffalo had gone.

> "Yet, it was not just the buffalo they missed. Elk were gone. Wolves and coyotes. Rabbits! When they put their minds to it the women realized that they had seen no four-leggeds at all since the spring. None! Absolutely no animals large or small. Whole villages of prairie dogs were silent...No animals? Ah, that caused the women to lie awake at night....

> "No company in the world.
> Things felt still and dirty, as if a nation had not washed for a very long time, as if they were sleeping in their own sweat...
> This was the start of the year of terrible hunger and loneliness. And maybe the loneliness was worse than the hunger...All human people began to feel solitary in the universe. Strangers."

This community, that common people in whom all people might see themselves, becomes the "controlling metaphor" of the novel as Wangerin descriptively shows what happens to a community when all its myths are exploded, its center forgotten, and the cosmos doesn't make sense. As the work explains, all sense of community is broken, all covenants are broken, and the world becomes chaotic and pointless - the people become bewildered.

> "They said: 'Wakan Tanka has turned away from us.'
>
> They said: 'Who sinned? Who is not confessing his sin?'
>
> They said: 'Where did Tatanka go? Why does he hate us now? Why did he leave us to die?'
>
> It was an empty land. A dead land...The earth cracked. The earth itself was dying."

Wangerin combines image after image of chaos, hunger and loneliness to enable the reader to sense the horror of a community without a center, without meaning, without hope. When finally Standing Hollow Horn discovers Red Day woman's death in childbirth, he cries: "Who could do such a thing!...So, so this is how we walk the black road! Everyone for himself, each one with little rules of his own. So! So!"

But Fire Thunder who is responsible for the condition of the world gazes in silence as the people ask: "What good are you now, Fire Thunder?"

These scenes parallel so closely the condition of the characters in The Book of Sorrows: "The creatures were cold; and now, at the returning of the Cock, it seemed that the Fimbul Winter would last forever. They were hopeless...And Pertelote had lost her will to care for or console the Animals. Not even her sweet voice sang faith to the souls, nor did she try to control their selfish behavior....So the Animals were left to their own devices, stricken and hopeless and cold, unnerved and hungry, despairing...Then into this troubled congregation of Animals there came a terrible word...that word was Death...No one deserves to die, but Black-Pale least of all. This is horrible! This is the confounding of everything right or good! This is wrong. Oh, this..." And in The Crying for a Vision, the simple-minded, kind and slant-eyed child whom the people called Red Day Woman stopped smiling...and as her baby cries, Standing Hollow Horn screams at Fire Thunder... "'Do you hear this baby crying? She is crying because of you! She is all sorrows come to life in a tiny baby! She is our hunger in the flesh..."

The Crying for a Vision is not developed chronologically with a simple straight-forward plot, but the sections are linked together symbolically with a section explaining the background of the images introduced in the preceding chapters and symbols and characters developed or explained by the flashbacks and historical renderings of the narrator. But, in spite of the lack of chronological ordering, the novel moves forward quickly, and the reader never feels confused because the symbols, characters and overriding myths of the Lacotas give the novel a tight unity. Each symbol and each character's actions are fully explained, and one realizes that each introduced detail, from the loss of Fire Thunder's eye, to the death of the Grandmother's husband, are integral to the wholeness of the story.

A brief look at some of the details of Wangerin's symbols in this work indicates the artistic control of the author over the narrator and the story.

Fire Thunder is first introduced as a mighty hunter, a "man like a single cottonwood tree standing alone midfield, tall and tough," and "slanting down his forehead and cheek in order to cover the left eye forever -- an otterskin headband." "Whoever had seen beneath the slash of the headband? Who knows what was hidden there? The right eye flashed like black obsidian; the left remained as mysterious as God...His jaw was of stone and perhaps his left eye was an eagle's beak!

"He fights in silence, the young men said. He fights in solitude. He never cries out and even when he is done he does not utter stories."

Later in the story the reader begins to understand the significance of this description. Fire Thunder's loss of eye is connected to a time when he was outwitted by a Crow Indian; and "One arrow hit his left eye, pierced it, and stuck there...And suddenly he (Fire Thunder) knew who was making that weird high sound, and he shivered with horror because it was himself. He, Fire Thunder, had been screaming through his nose like an infant. Hokshi cala! Oh, a cold heat took his heart in that moment, the white rage of humiliation, and he began struggling to perform prodigious tasks..."

But when he lost his eye, "He felt no pain. He felt instead a mortal shame. Fire Thunder had seen his sight go away on the point of an enemy's arrow, the eye ripped from his head, and he saw himself thereby disfigured. Monstrous and dishonored..."

By the time Fire Thunder returns to the Lacota, he is filled with hate, "hatred so cold and sweet that it felt like delight, and in his face it became a mechanical clam, and...he was peaceful...

"And thus he returned transfigured.

"Mute and mysterious, from that day forward he puzzled the people he moved among...He told no stories regarding himself. He sang no songs.

"Over his left eye he wore an otterskin headband ever thereafter, like a slash across his forehead. He never removed it."

Part of the significance of this headband and what it symbolizes begins to be explained in this section: "Never again did the people see the whole of this warrior-hunter: a piece was concealed forever." Not only do the people never see the physical part of this warrior, the other gentle side (as developed by his sister Red Day Woman) is also hidden from view (even from Fire Thunder himself.) And Fire Thunder only sees material reality from this time on -- the spiritual, invisible reality he is blind to. And the silence he imposes upon himself as he buries his shame deep inside makes others speculate about who he is, about what laws he obeys and what power lies beneath his hidden eye. So the very covering of his shame becomes his source of strength and inside him "hatred resolves itself into an elegant thing within him...and he would never love again." And as Wangerin later reveals, from this time forward Fire Thunder is a powerful evil force and "worships and obeys no one except himself." And as the Indian nations begin to recognize the truth of his evil they said: "Then, then he is wakan shica, that evil which is equal to Wakan Tanka, wickedness in proportion to God." And just as the Lacota legend tells (which Wangerin narrates earlier in the story), "the white wolf swallowed the sun...then the whole earth suffered dark and cold and misery. The circle was broken. Every creature went hungry and none could serve another -- that was the Black Road; so Shunkmanitu Tanka speculates that Fire Thunder did not ask, did not serve...but walked with a haughty spirit, silent inside himself as if soon he will want to swallow the sun." And so as the story progresses, this is what Fire Thunder does, and blood- shed, hunger and death come to the people and to the creatures and the earth because of him. And the Sacred Cottonwood Tree is dropped, the Mystery Dance is canceled and Fire Thunder (as tall as the single cottonwood tree himself, and thereby replacing the sacred one,) leads the people into war and death and down the Black Road.

Thus evil and sin and its consequences can be seen through this novel, and Wangerin as artist allows the reader to experience the consequences of the breaking of the sacred circle, the losing of the myths, and enables him to see how everything that gives coherence to a culture can be broken by one person who sins, then hides his pain and turns it inward into hatred and anger but who exerts "such influence on a nation that he alone prevails...and the Lacota do not dance...rather, they go on the warpath, obeying his rules and his spirit." And these people "swell in pride forgetting that the door of the sweat lodge is small in order to force a man to bow low and to indicate that he is nothing next to Wakan Tanka unto whom he prays"...but the older Holy Men knew that this sin would end in the death and destruction of the nation for "how could a nation prosper if it did not honor Wakan Tanka or humble itself before him in prayer and sacrifice? Well, it could not."

Wangerin creates this powerful evil force against which a seemingly weak, misfit of the culture must stand: Waskn Mani. The symbols of circles, light, darkness, sacred items of the culture, stars, ghosts, lotus flowers, etc., all work together, all enable the novel to speak truth on its own without the moralistic intrusion of the author. And all the symbols developed are part of the climax of the novel as the headband of Fire Thunder has to be removed before he can choose to humble himself before Waskn Mani to save his people from total destruction. And the earth drum which warned Fire Thunder not to sin and was not listened to by him, once again sounds, and this time listened to as "Fire Thunder hears it for the first time, and he begins to dance to its rhythm." The sacred circle and dance are begun again, the animals return, and the red and blue days are sent by Wakan Tanka once again.

Sin, destruction, repentance, relationship to the earth, listening to God's creation and its creatures, love, sacrifice, death and rebirth are all shown in this novel, and the reader experiences, as he does in The Orphean Passages, the events of these themes, as well as understands them. And this Lacota world, because of the artistic skills of Wangerin, truly becomes that "common people in whom all peoples might see themselves...and this vision is a rich analogue for the relationship any people of genuine faith experiences with creation and the Creator." And as Wangerin explains, the Lacota mystery world, at least in part, corresponds to the shape of the Gospel. Virginia Owens explains in her article, "Walter Wangerin and the Cosmic Equation," "Both the Lacota and the Christian world agree that we are to see through the natural world to the spiritual rather than separating them into a dual universe. Creation is a lens we use to focus on the holy. Second, both worlds conceive of sin in similar ways -- putting one in the center or the individual turning in on himself. Third, pain is the path to healing because it is a participant in the suffering of the universe, and causes one both to pray and to humble oneself before the sufferings of the Redeemer. 'Christ's own passion,' C.S. Lewis said, 'makes true all myths which reveal the necessity of sacrifice as the shape of reality.'" (Virginia Owens)

One can truly see through this story of Wangerin's to the truth and the experience of Christ's death and sacrifice, and the reader can find in this story the conditions of our own world and our own lives where evil seems so powerful, and we can't see the falconer any longer, and things are flying apart in chaos. And this work and Wangerin's others, like the myth of Orpheus he retells in The Orphean Passages, allow us to descend to the underworld, the darkness, and the emptiness of life and culture without songs, or myths, or stories. And the bewilderment of each of us and each character of Wangerin's increases as the sufferings and deaths make no sense, and Chauntecleer never crows the crows again as he mourns the loss of his innocence, and of love, and of God; and Fire Thunder in silence sits with his head bowed, his great arms folded over his knees, the left arm ravaged with Red Scars..." Always one could feel the presence of mighty Fire Thunder even without seeing him - but this time there seemed to be no presence at all -- Emptyness."

But, as in all of his works, so in The Crying for a Vision Wangerin does not leave the reader in despair, although the sorrow and evil seem all powerful. Waskn Mani, because of his deep love for his people, suffers intense pain at their suffering, and his grandmother gives him the sacred pipe of his grandfather, Black Elk, and he is sent out to a sacred place to "pray to Wakan Tanka for a vision that can save the people. If someone does not save the hoop of the world, everyone will die."

Although Waskn Mani sees himself as unworthy of praying

for the people, the thunder commands him to "Wachin ksapa yo! Be attentive." And he is given the vision that will save his people and Fire Thunder. All of the sacred images of the Lacota are employed by Wangerin to achieve the artistic intensity of this vision quest, and to complete the circle of the earth: the buffalo woman, the sacred pipe, the sacred mountain. All of these symbols which have been developing slowly in Waskn Mani throughout the years are "microcosmicly telescoped into his vision quest," and Waskn Mani is attentive to creatively seeing the symbols in all life, and thus, he can bring the vision back to the people to repair the sacred hoop. Death, self-will, evil, repentance, sacrifice, new birth, are all reflected in these masterfully woven Lacota myths, and each reader sees his/her relationship with the creation and the Creator reflected in the actions. And hope is reborn in the Lacota and in the reader: "The Lacota once again danced in the sacred circle and they sang new songs and they cried in sorrow and they laughed in happiness. And the animals were back."

Although this work has a simple surface which closely resembles the oral tradition of literature, as the story unfolds, the internal complexity and underlying Lacota symbols begin to emerge so that even seemingly simple, descriptive scenes "speak" to the underlying meaning. None of the introduced descriptions are inserted except as they add to the symbolism and the complexity whether it is Red Day Woman as a child, the burnt scar on the face of the mountain, the loss of an eye by Fire Thunder, the names of characters (for example: Standing Hollow Horn - empty of self to speak for God), individual phrases spoken at the beginning and referred to over and over (Wachin ksapa yo: Be attentive); the water lilies -- all contribute to the beauty and the mythic quality of the story. Wangerin has carefully chosen each myth, each Lacota legend, to create single fictional characters from a composite of people, and he invents details and characters in order to communicate the deeper spirit of the story. And he "tightens the pace of human life accordingly" giving a sense of kairos or God's time when chronological time needs to be transcended and eternity needs to be felt. The cosmos of the story thus, uses seen reality and the invisible reality most people miss, and brings them together so that the reader can also learn to be attentive to the smallest details of life which might be "carrying the news of heaven down to him."

In his style he integrates simple and complex sentences to

control the emphasis and the pace of the story and has abrupt interruptions in thought to force the reader to pay attention. Many times, the very simple sentences reveal deeply symbolic but sharply drawn images:

> "The night was cold and empty.
> This is the way the war ended.
> The warriors just came home."

The greatest foreshadowing occurs in the short interruptions. As the Rabbits speak:

> "Look! Like a four-legged! Right away he moves walking!
> We know. We were there. We saw his nativity.
> And we have kept our eye on him ever since.
> We expect great things from that boy."

Wangerin's variety in sentences, descriptive details, contrasts of light and darkness, depersonalized narrator, and combination of fantastic and realistic elements, all combine to produce a work that uses the best elements of the oral tradition, fairy tales, and myths. The story holds the reader's attention and is entertaining, but "it also stimulates one's imagination and helps the reader clarify his/her emotions." As Bettelheim states: "The fairy tale hero proceeds for a time in isolation and is in touch with primitive things - a tree, an animal, nature, and...he, although sometimes groping in dark, is, through the course of his life guided step by step and given help when it is needed....In fairy tales evil is as omnipresent as virtue...and the propensities for good and evil are present in every human. It is this duality which poses the moral problem and requires the struggle to solve it....In many fairy tales this evil often is temporarily in the ascendancy." (Bettelheim) All of these fairy tale elements are present in The Crying for a Vision, but with these are added mythical elements which unite these real life situations and the conflict between good and evil with the mythical experiences of rigorous self-sacrifice and "supra-human" images of heroism which point to the ultimate truths underlying the surface conflicts. The sacrifice at the end of The Crying for a Vision clearly illustrates one of the mythical elements of the work: "Oiyan! Here is a boy above us! An enormous boy, a beautiful, burning boy! His flesh was pure light, his body the rock of the mountain, his cheekbones two cliffs too high for climbing...And then we saw some lightning ripple at the boy's mouth...the serious lightning forked from his mouth in a long arc to the stone at the foot of the mountain." In spite of the mythical portrayal of Moves Walking, his choices made throughout his life have allowed this change and transfiguration, and the reader is prepared for a "super-human sacrifice." Wangerin never leaves reality too far behind, for even at the ending, it is the choice made by Fire Thunder which will save or lose his people. It is not a forced, deus ex machina, solution. This choice is set forth by Moves Walking as he speaks to Fire Thunder:

> "Once what you chose to do began their (the Lacota
>   people's) dying.
> Now what you refuse to do will finish it and rub out all
>   the people. All the people!...If you do not kill me,
>   the people will perish."

The life of the people is dependent not only on Waskn Mani's willing sacrifice, but on Fire Thunder's willingness to humble himself and to be truthful.

Wangerin invites the reader into the cosmos of his work, and it has such internal integrity and consistency that the reader understands deeply the truth of the story even though some of the elements are unreal and fantastic. Like all excellent fairy tales and myths, this work depicts realistically yet symbolically the essential decisions facing each human. Although Wangerin's work "points the way to a better future" for the Lacota, he concentrates in the work on the process of change, rather than on the bliss to be enjoyed. Thus, once the sacrifice is made, Wangerin quickly ends the work as the buffalo come back, the famine is over, and they dance in a sacred circle once again. The center of the Lacota world once again holds, and the red and blue days return.

Chapter IX.

FAIRY TALES, EVIL, AND TRUTH IN ART

Shaping our lives with Words of Power

FAIRY TALES, EVIL, AND TRUTH IN ART

"Life will go on
As long as there is someone
To sing, to dance, to tell stories, and to listen."

Oren Lyons

"Hans Andersen's stories, though simple on the surface, contain a precise and tender perception of personal development. They are honest about the hard encounter with the 'real world' -- honest about evil and the tendency to evil in each of us. Andersen didn't coddle me, the 'me' who was revealed within his fairy tales. He didn't sweeten the bitter facts which I already knew regarding myself. But he offered me hope, for in his tales even when evil has been chosen, forgiveness may follow -- therein lies extraordinary hope. Never, never does Andersen compromise the truth of human experience for childish ears...Hans Andersen has persuaded me of optimism, not the Pollyanna sugar which merely sweetens the facts of evil and suffering, danger and death. I would soon reject such optimism as fraudulent -- even as a child I would. It would leave no print upon my personality. But Andersen's optimism both sees and redeems the evil. We travel through it, not around it, and I am impressed forever."

Wangerin's fiction shows the influence of Andersen's stories upon his theory and style. Many of his works are in the form of fairy tales, and the characters are fantastically drawn, but in each, Wangerin "gets across that a struggle against severe difficulties in

109

life is unavoidable, is an intrinsic part of human existence -- but that if one does not shy away from but steadfastly meets unexpected and often unjust hardships, one masters the obstacles and at the end emerges victorious. Evil is as omnipresent as virtue, and the propensities for both are present in every human." (Bettelheim)

Thus his earliest written children's book begins "Once upon a time there lived a man and a woman in a potato house....One thing only troubled their lives: they had no children though they wished with all their hearts for sons and daughters. The man in his field and the woman at home were lonely." After setting the fairy tale tone at the opening, Wangerin then begins to delve into the evil and good in this world as the story unfolds, and the man and his wife have four children, all except one manifesting self-centeredness, vanity and pride. The fourth child, unlike the first three, was "short, stumpy, a little too chubby, too low in the waist, her fingers both clumsy and thick...and the couple protected her the best they could." But evil is revealed when her brother "Pine grew proud and called her 'short;' Oak, impatient pushed her aside and told her she was too fat; Rose would smile as cold as ice; and Thistle would cry in her hands." And the conflict between good and evil is established as the Mother would tell her children: "Thistle is our daughter...she should not cry. The Lord loves the little, and the Good will walk in his way. Pine, she should not cry; Oak and Rose, she shouldn't be made to cry, no, not so much as a tear."

Wangerin, like Andersen, does not spare Thistle hurts and tears, does not change her into a physically beautiful person to shame her brothers and sisters, but forces her to face powerful evil and suffering and to conquer them. As Thistle's parents, brothers and sister are overcome by the powerful evil as they rely only on their external beauty or strengths to conquer it, Thistle alone is left with her tears -- alone is left with her helplessness. "Six were four, and four but two, and two no more than one. Poor Thistle, poor youngest of them all, left alone in the potato house. 'Can you do nothing by cry?' she said to herself. 'No nothing, but cry.'....'I wish I were tall,' she wept, but she was short. 'I wish I were strong.' But she was weak. 'Dear God, I wish I were beautiful.' But she was a plain sort, with nothing of value and nothing to use in the fight against Pudge, nothing, no nothing but tears.'

"Poor Thistle. She stumbled from the house...All the world

was a lonely place. All the sky was grey, and all the ground gone stony, and all the cockleburs clutched at her as she passed by. And the forest did not love her."

What a realistic fairy tale Wangerin weaves as he forces this young girl to face her aloneness, her emptiness. Wangerin doesn't make it easier for her, and he doesn't sugar-coat the emptiness and evil in the world for the reader. For each of us, children or adults, need to recognize the evil, name the deaths, and learn to travel through them to hope. And Wangerin through all of his works asks his readers to face their fears for "fear keeps one humble and makes us listen....The world wants to escape from fear...but when I refuse to name evil, to face my loneliness and fears, I meet a safe Jesus, and the trouble is that a safe Jesus never saved the world. A safe Jesus would have never been able to face the suffering and defeat of the cross."

So Wangerin, like Andersen, wants the reader to face his fears, isolation and death -- these are the fertile soil in which hope, love, and resurrection can grow. As Thistle faces her emptiness she cries out to a "hunch-backed witch" who meets her:

> "'Oh, Mother, What can I do? Pudge has eaten all the height and strength and beauty of the world. What is left? What is left?'"

But Wangerin does not leave Thistle in despair. She has nothing to lose now but her self and, unlike her brothers and sisters, gladly accepts the kiss from the ugly witch, not knowing that from this humble self-sacrifice would spring the defeat of the evil. As the story ends, and Thistle offers herself to be eaten by Pudge, the transformation occurs, and the evil Pudge is destroyed: "And out of the hole came Thistle! And next came Rose and Oak and Pine alive, and happy, and well. And then the good man and his wife stepped out....And who was it they looked for? Why for Thistle.

"What a hugging was in the potato house that day. The family threw arms around each other and danced, and laughed, and cried; and no one said 'No' to the tears anymore, but everyone wept them together. For by her crying Thistle had brought them to life, and by her loving they were saved."

Each of Wangerin's short fictional works, whether told in the fantastic language of fairy tales or told in the realistic tone of the inner city life, reveals the same themes: loneliness, pride, sin, evil, sacrifice, death and resurrection, the very themes that are woven throughout the stories of the Bible, and thus, form Wangerin's perception of the "true reality" -- the many times unseen reality of love, beauty, joy and resurrection behind the evil and death.

His first book of short stories, <u>Ragman and Other Cries of Faith,</u> continues his themes but with a mixture of realistic and fantastic elements all intertwined to enable the reader to see the sorrows of the world and to see through them to God and hope. As he states in his Invocation to the collection of stories: "Turning to the city, do I turn from you? No, my Lord, for you are in the city. In all of the affairs of human kind, you are there. You were not ashamed to be born of a woman, flesh like hers and mine, troubled as she and I by all the bruises of that flesh. You emptied yourself to enter the city, and though your coming may not make it good, it makes you cry, and there you are. In the oily streets, damp with rain and human sin, lit by a single light, I see your face reflected." Throughout this work and all of his works, the face of God is seen in unlikely messengers: Arthur Forte, the lady at the supermarket, Robert, the Baglady, Miz Lil -- all messengers of God speaking to us through the stories -- not preaching at us but evoking from us heartfelt cries of recognition both of guilt, suffering and despair and of hope and purpose.

But as Wangerin states, for us to see them and to see ourselves, since we cannot see for ourselves, he tells us stories: "I tell them a thousand stories, Lord. For the city is active, and you are acting in it, always; and activity's a story. I tell them about you by telling them the story...And I use the forms they understand: drama, poetry, essay, fable, and form whereby the words may cry the Word."

His stories cause us to see our rags, to see our helplessness, and to see God's love and forgiveness for us, and, after reading them, we "lower our heads and trembling for all we have seen, we walk up to the Ragman. We tell him our name with shame, for we are sorry figures next to him. And we take off our clothes and say to him: 'Dress me.' And he dresses us. My Lord, he puts new rags on us, and we are wonders beside him. The Ragman, the Ragman, the Christ."

Wangerin further explains the power of and reasons behind his stories, in an essay in <u>The Ragman</u> volume on "Preaching." "The shape of our preaching most shapes our God. And what is the shape of our preaching today? Why, it is the shape of the classroom, teaching. And teaching is always one step removed from experience and from the 'real.' It is an activity of the mind -- this God has been abstracted from the rest of the Christian's experience....But God chooses to touch us whole, not only in our minds; so tell stories, ye preachers of God. Humble yourselves to make of yourself a parable.

"Because when you do that, you invite, as well, the wholeness of the hearers. Then not only their analytic minds, but their laughter shall be in the pew...and their bodies, their sympathy, their emotions, their distress, their inadequacy, their maleness and femaleness, their parenthood - their experience! You will be inviting them as people into a relationship with you...And then...if God's temple is their experience, they shall know him immanent indeed. Nothing is not the stuff of story. All of the senses participate...The stories of experiences (themselves becoming experiences for the hearers) prepare the people to see God approach them through experience."

Wangerin honestly, sometimes painfully honestly, presents the world of experiences to his readers, and portrays life wholly not ignoring the unanswerable problems and ills, but he never forgets to portray this world of experiences as a world where God's love, God's forgiveness, and God's healing are always in the background, many times hidden but always there. Wangerin makes a covenant with his reader not to tell a lie as truth but to always draw his stories from carefully observed reality. He, as he states, will name "reality rightly and carefully and will not deceive his reader," but he does take risks with his reader. He allows the stories to stand on their own, and he names things in new ways, and allows his stories to work on his reader so that the reader experiences the reality by abiding in the work of art for a time. The reader is invited to enter the story, and when the story is "truthful" and works, he brings the experience of this reality back with him into his own world.

Many of Wangerin's characters are powerless, alone and afraid because they have listened to false stories or have allowed someone else to tell their story for them: "You are stupid; you are ugly. You are useless." And through his stories, Wangerin brings about events that enable the characters and the readers to go behind the false stories that have been told them to hear their true stories. By embracing and respecting their real stories (as seen through the wholistic vision of God) they develop a sense of pity, self-worth and empowerment. For in Wangerin's stories it is Jesus who asks, "How are you?" And if we can see the false self by which we sustain our contemptible self and "allow it to die and admit that we are lonely or afraid or ugly or hurtful, then we would know that he has loved us all along -- that he loves us not because we are lovable but because he is love....And here is the power of his love, that it makes ugliness beautiful! To be loved of God is to be loved indeed." (The Ragman)

Wangerin believes strongly in this God who cries out with the "trumpet voice": "I love a child. But she is afraid of me. Then how can I come to her, to feed and to heal her by my love?"

These powerful sacred stories of Wangerin's begin the process of making us open to hearing God's voice of love. "They move us; they get us thinking about what is important; they communicate through symbol and metaphor deep truths about the mysteries of life." ("Sacred Stories," p. II) Upon hearing Wangerin's stories, even if we don't understand the message intellectually, "we are aware that some profound lesson has been imparted." Not all of Wangerin's stories have a religious context and surface, but beneath the surface of all of his works, deeper, spiritual meanings are always present. Like the parables of Christ which show how God was present in everyday life, with the images of a woman kneading dough or searching for a lost coin, so Wangerin's tale of inner city life and daily happenings remind us that the divine appears in the most ordinary realities. Wangerin sees God in the details of life, and, thus, even when he is telling one's personal or family stories, these become religious events and enable the reader to understand the immanence of God and teach us as readers to see him in the mundane, dailyness of our lives.

Each of Wangerin's personal stories of his children and ministry takes small daily events -- the losing of one's temper, the interruptions of one's work -- and sees through these to the hidden workings of God. An excellent illustration of this is "Mary at Fourteen: A Hug as Holy as the Ocean" in which Wangerin relates: "I snapped at you last week. I could justify my anger, I suppose, historically account reasons, could conclude our dispute with my own parental righteousness, and so be done.

"But then I would miss your hug, and my forgiveness, and the face of Jesus in my daughter's face -- and so would not be done at all. Self-righteousness is a miserly conclusion. And I cherish your hug.

"God has given us nothing more practical and miraculous at once than forgiveness, nothing better for cleansing the sinner and curing his victim -- no, nothing save Jesus, whose face I found in your face, beautiful Mary, whom I love with all my heart. You hugged me, and the cliffs rose noble all around me, and California Christiandom declared: 'Amen.'"

Or the event described in his short works may be as small as a seven-year-old boy touching the wing of a cicada, unknowingly damaging it. Then when realizing what he had done crying out: "Oh, No! I had hurt the wing. I sucked a panicky breath. I couldn't undo the thing that I had done...The beautiful green liquid in her wing -- that was blood...That was her blood...I felt two moods intensely. I couldn't abolish wonder at the beauty of that deep green drop of blood. Yet, I cried to realize that to render such a beauty had cost the life of a living thing. She spent everything she had...And this is what I say today...Christ on the cross is more beautiful than anything -- for extreme is the cost of extremest beauty. What I witnessed on that summer's day at seven was the sign of sacrifice."

Wangerin's awareness of small, specific details, his careful listening to the stories of his childhood, his careful observation of life, these all add to the intensity of his style. There is no event that is too small to miss the scrutiny of this writer, and even in the most unlovable person in his stories, traces of beauty and of God's love and sacrifice are seen. Although he minutely details the physical realities of his stories, these details serve to eliminate the distance between the reader and the narrator and enable the reader to enter wholly into the narrator's world and to not be afraid to listen. Wangerin creates his stories' cosmos out of the daily details of the reader's world enabling us as readers to lose our convenient dividing of the events of our lives into sacred and non-sacred events. All events are sacred -- all can be epiphanies through which God can speak to us, and Wangerin effectively creates these moments of encounter with God in our mundane world.

As he states in his short work "Edification/Demolition": "You say: 'But how can I serve the Lord? I'm not important. What I do is common and of little consequence.'

"But I say to you: Every time you meet another human being you have the opportunity. It's a chance at holiness. For you will do one of two things, then. Either you will build him up, or you will tear him down. Either you will acknowledge that he is, or you will make him sorry that he is -- sorry, at least that he is there, in front of you....And I say to you: There are no useless, minor meetings...There are no pointless lives."

Wangerin's short works are meant to be parables to us, comforts to us, symbols through which we can transcend our own chaotic lives, nearsightedness, and chronology to see behind them to God. And since these stories "involve people whole -- enticing personal commitment by the desire to hear the ending -- then we are more likely to truly see and truly hear the quiet workings of love, beauty, and purpose. The stories of experience (themselves becoming experiences for the hearers) prepare the people to see God approach them through experience.

"When Mary Ellen Phillips heard Wangerin's story of 'Lily,' she told it to her niece in Nevada, who suffered from muscular dystrophy, and the niece chuckled to hear it. But when that niece's friend died in a cruel accident -- none could comfort her, not her parents, not her pastor, none. But Mary Ellen went into the bedroom where the child was crying, and prayed to God for words to say, but had none. But then her niece said, 'Tell me the story of Lily.'"

We as Wangerin's readers and as humans don't want doctrine, or promises, we want expressions of God's love, forgiveness and resurrection. Potter doesn't need doctrines of faith, he needs the experience of faith, and thus the Phoenix becomes his experience. And he is then urged to go and "comfort his mother. Now is the time to share the resurrection. Or would you keep such a wonder to yourself?"

J.R.R. Tolkien in his essay "On Fairy-Stories," glories in the imaginations' "freedom from the domination of observed fact." Tolkien stressed that separateness because he believed that the further stories are removed from our world, the better they can convey a "sudden glimpse of the underlying reality of truth." Thus Tolkien carefully distanced his stories from the world's of everyday reality. (Schakel, p. 127) But Wangerin always grounds his characters and his fictions (even his fantasies) in the everyday reality and the knowable world. Behind all of the knowable groundings in the everyday life are the controlling myths and stories of the Christian faith, but these are always stabilized in the knowable world. Wangerin would agree with C. S. Lewis' statements in the conclusion of the passage in The Pilgrim's Regress: "For salvation one needs both 'real things' (the actual carnation, crucifixion and resurrection) and myth (which shows the significance of those things). And both are emphasized by the Divine voice's words (in Pilgrim's Regress): For this end I made your senses (to see and taste real bread and wine) and for this end your imagination (to bring out the significance that they are the blood and body of a dying and yet living God)." (Schakel, p. 125)

So Wangerin gives us the physical world which can be known by the senses, grounds his stories in this world, so that at they are not alien to us, and then shows through his choice of descriptions the signifying aspect of these events. His fantasies and allegorical works always refer to and point to the world of physical events, so that both incarnation and transcendence can occur.

Thus, in <u>Branta and the Golden Stone</u> the descriptions are vivid and physical even though the parable points beyond the visible world to the incarnation of Christ.

> "Once there was a girl who lived alone on the northernmost island of all the world.
> "She lived in a cottage by a lake. The lake was ice for most of the year, banked with white snow. Her Father had built the cottage long ago. It had two rooms, and a fireplace, a table, a chair, a little window that faced the lake, and in each room a little bed....Her name was Branta."

As the story continues many other physical descriptions are given of the cold, the death and confessed sin of her father, the isolation and near death of the geese. But the symbolic/allegorical aspect of Branta becomes apparent as she ponders how she can rescue the stranded geese since they are afraid of her.

> "'Wait,' she called. 'I want to help you.'
> "But they were afraid of her! They were as scared of Branta as they were of the storm....'Come, with me,' she begged. 'You'll die out here.'
> "But it was no good.
> "So then, thought Branta, maybe I could scare them into the cottage!...But they ran further and further away."

Just as we run from knowledge of ourselves, from God, and his love and warmth, so these geese ran from Branta. And just as God throughout history has tried to draw humans to himself through his shikinal glory, his power, his tears, yet humans continued to flee from him. He had to devise a way that He could speak to us without scaring us, so "Branta ponders: 'Baby King, I want to be a goose.'"

Then as she becomes one like them, the geese stand up and follow her into the warmth of the cottage...."And so it was they survived...For this was the truth of the Golden Stone, the length of time and the fullness of sacrifice."

When this story is paralleled to Wangerin's "An Advent Monologue," the allegorical elements of <u>Branta and the Golden Stone</u> become even more apparent.

> "I love a child.
> But she is afraid of me.
> I want to help this child, so terribly in need of help. For she is hungry...she is cold...she is lonely all day long...I love this child.
> But she is afraid of me.
> Then how can I come to her, to feed and to heal her by my love?
> I know what I will do.
> I'll make the woman herself my door - and by her body enter into her life...
> All that she suffered, the hurts at the hands of men, shall be transfigured by my being: I'll make good come out of evil; I am the good come out of evil.
> I am her Lord, who loves this woman.
> ...Look! Look...I am doing a new thing -- and don't you perceive it? I am coming among you - a baby.
> And my name shall be Emanuel."

> "Out of experience rises the Word in order to lodge in experience once again. And story is experience communicated. Story is Word and experience abiding each within the other."

Although Wangerin's shorter works treat such serious themes, he uses humor, exaggeration, and reversals to add entertainment and humor to his stories. He is able to gain emotional distance and laugh at himself, and he enables us as his readers to see our shortcomings, our sins, but to laugh at ourselves as God brings good even from our errors. And by reducing our sins and hurts to something we ultimately laugh at, we can manage the pain. As he states in "Shaping the Child's Universe":

> "There is violence here (in Little Claus and Big Claus): horse killings, grandma killings, old men sent to heaven, and a great rich fool apparently drowned. But the violence accords with nightmares of my own...And the violence is funny! I listen and laugh till tears run down my cheeks and my father laughs too.

What is happening? Violence is being reduced to something manageable; and because I am the one laughing at it, scorning it, recognizing the blustering silliness of it, then I am larger than it, capable of triumphing over it. This story does not deny the monster in me or the cruelties of the general society, it empowers me....Hans Christian Andersen has persuaded me of optimism, a tough and abiding optimism."

In <u>Elizabeth and the Water Troll</u>, Wangerin creates a recognizable fairy tale character, the Troll who lives in the well called Despair. But his description of the Troll is unique:

"Ah, the Troll, the very reason why the well is called Despair! What shall we say of him? What is the truth and not a lie?

"Well, he isn't a mole, because he's too much like a man. He frowns like a man; yet he can't be a man exactly, because he digs in the darkness and shrinks from the light. His arms are long and powerful. He has claws on his fingers and fangs in his mouth and green in his eyes, and he leaps from the ledges inside his well as lightly as a cat. His fur is thick; his back is hunched; his whiskers are wet -- and always his brow is frowning since always he's trying to think, and thinking is hard for the Troll who isn't a man exactly."

A young, innocent girl who has lost her Mother to death and has lost her trust in love and her hope, a Troll in the well of Despair, a loving Father, and a prejudiced self-centered town -- these all form the key elements of this imaginative fairy tale. Despair, death, darkness, fear, prejudice and murder -- all powerful evil pitted against innocence, love, healing tears, sacrifice, and hope. Wangerin doesn't minimize the despair over death, the darkness and ugliness of the Troll nor the prejudiced evil of the townspeople, and he makes the ending of the tale dependent upon the willing choosing of the characters to act, to hate, to fear, to love. And the Troll at the beginning is "frowning on account of a difficult thought, how to make one sad heart happy." But the realism and optimism of Wangerin are apparent in this fairy tale, and his belief in the tremendous power of despair, death, and evil as well as his belief in the power of love, hope, resurrection are intricately linked throughout. As the Troll sacrifices himself to save Elizabeth's life, "the tears run from his green, green eyes, but he does not groan....And then he kneels in front of a weeping man (Elizabeth's Father) and gently he unwraps his hair, and there is Elizabeth, safe and pale, and crying, too: And that makes three in tears.

"...The child gazes at the dying Troll. She's grieving.

"Nay·Beth, Nay, don't cry."

As the Troll gives back the tortoiseshell combs to Elizabeth, the love of the three for one another is seen through the tears, and the Troll "has thought his thought and shall never frown again. He looks on the child with an infinite peace...." In this story Wangerin brings about hope and love even as the main characters cry and in the midst of death, but the love of each for the other overcomes despair and prejudice.

In many of Wangerin's other shorter works, the reader finds himself laughing at the situations, at Wangerin's or the Narrator's self-consciousness and embarrassment, yet even in these works the power of selfishness, despair and evil is never ignored, but like Wangerin as a child did, so we can power over the evil through the laughter, and we are empowered to hope in the midst of overwhelming evil.

Although "The Baglady" is concerned with poverty, our ignorance of the poor, our failure to recognize their gifts to us and to recognize God's angels among us, at the end we find Wangerin and ourselves laughing at God's methods for getting our attention.

"Indeed, God was in this baglady. Whether the LaSalle Church was aware of that or not, I was.

"And yet I could have explained the awe in me, if awe was all there was.... What I could not have explained...was that my mouth kept smearing into a grin and my chest kept pumping toward an outright laugh....

"Angels, Yes indeed! But when angels descend from Cabrini Green and not from condominiums, they don't bathe first; they don't approve themselves with pieties first; they do not fit the figment of Christian imagination; they prophesy as they are and expect us to honor them whole.

"I wanted so badly to laugh, because God was roaring a wonderful thunder, surely. The baglady had been a joke. Yes -- and the joke was God's....

"The messenger of God was cracked. And so was I, to her shrewd eye. Oh, we were a subversive pair in this rational middle mix Americans at worship....

"And God was pounding his thighs and weeping
with laughter, surely."

Many of Wangerin's shorter works end with this divine
laughter as the reader and the narrator see through his and our
many times absurd attempts at controlling our lives. Even while
the Pastor Wangerin in "Miz Lil" is talking to Miz Lil about the
death of her beloved husband, he states:

"The old woman is giggling. She clutches my knee:

"'Pastor! I'm sorry, Pastor,' she giggles right mer-
rily. 'You make such a pitiful picture...I'm sorry. Hee
Hee! That's a long time to be sitting on the pity pot!'

"Miz Lil is trying very hard to control the sudden
hilarity in her throat, or else to make it respectful. She
fails both ways...She wants to toss her head with the
laughter. Instead she takes both of my hands in her
own and squeezes them....'And God quit frowning long
before you quit messing up. And me, I just forgot it,
Pastor!' Miz Lil is shaking, full of apology, full of delight
at once...and I am chuckling too....'Oh, my Pastor!' she
squeaks, 'What a terrible waste of devotion!'"

Each of Wangerin's stories delights in life, understands and
accurately depicts the evil, but once the healing and the evil is
understood, and forgiveness is received, the reader can laugh at
the evil and sin so that they become manageable. And we can
learn to accept forgiveness, healing, and to become little children
again delighting in God's presence and love. Katie Andraski stated that "Grace is God drawing you through a story. Wangerin
invites his readers to see how God's strange grace operates in
action and character. And when he tells his stories...their innocence
and grace do indeed draw readers through to God." (Andraski)

Wangerin is intensely honest and revealing in his stories
because "you can be honest if you know that you are forgiven. If
you're scared that you're not forgiven you don't tell anyone anything. But because you are forgiven you are free to continue in this
world without fear of judgment, or contempt, or mockery. If you
are forgiven, you can be more honest about the sin that is over.

"Anytime I write or tell stories on myself, and refer to my sinfulness or my foolishness, it's not a story which is not over. It's
not a story that is in the middle. It's a story that is done. The completion was in forgiveness." ("Frontline Ministry")

His short stories teach, evoke responses from us, expose our ignorance and pride, face the powerful evil in the world, and yet comfort us. "they offer us the 'felt' experience of the world with its negative and positive powers and of the needs, desires and frustrations of humans. It is the sort of acquaintance with the world and humans that every Christian who is attempting to trust God totally and to love appropriately must have if one's response to God's love is to come from the heart and not from the top of the head....Many times our own experiences with our fellow humans is so stereotyped and patterned that we seldom see beneath the clichés of surface relationships." (Sallie TeSellie) Wangerin goes beneath the clichés and in the honesty and hope of his stories comforts much "as a parent comforts a child. Through his stories people are relieved of confusion -- not as though their lives were explained to them intellectually and they understood, but rather as though a loving and powerful parent came and put arms around them, and they were comforted." ("Telling Tales")

This comforting is exactly what Wangerin does in his children's work, <u>In the Beginning there was no Sky</u>:

> "Little child,
> Yesterday I saw you crying...
> Come here, little child.
> Sit close to me and do not cry.
> God loves you even more than I do, and God knew that darkness could scare little children....Oh he performed marvels to keep you safe from fears and loneliness. Listen, listen to me, and learn why you don't need to cry...
>
> "This is a true story, child. Tomorrow go out and look at the world so you will see its truth; for there is the sky and the garden and the creatures the Lord God made for you. Will you feel lonely or sad or afraid again? Perhaps. And perhaps one day I'll tell you the story of why we feel such things...
>
> "As for now, sleep, sleep, my weary child, all peacefully -- because you lie in the lap of God."

Chapter X.

THE BOOK OF GOD

THE BOOK OF GOD

This, then, is the story that was told through the years and the centuries and the millennia to come... When the disciples disobeyed the priests and contin-ue to tell the story...the high priest would arrest them...But always upon their release they continued to tell the story anyway...James, the first disciple to die for telling the story, was beheaded...

Nevertheless, the story still was told.

Among those who persecuted the followers of Jesus was a Pharisee...But then the story that he strove to abolish rose up and overwhelmed him, becoming his only reality...Then, he too, began to tell the story...And the Church has continued after the written scriptures end. And the story has been told for two thousand years...Countless are the languages in which the story still is told. Innumerable the hearts that have been shaped by it.

from The Book of God

With Wangerin's theories of story and the power of telling true stories, it was only natural that his latest work would be a retelling of the stories of the Christian Scriptures, the source of true myth to this author. And so in his lengthy book, The Book of God, Wangerin uses the entire Christian Bible as his source for story, characters, and truth. Like all of his writing, Wangerin is concerned both with the literary quality of the telling and with his adherence to the truth of the original stories. And like his theory of story telling expressed in <u>The Crying for a Vision</u>, he accepts the storyteller's license to alter event and character in recounting a historical incident, for he believes that the meaning and the effect of the story take precedence over a record keeping sense of history. So Wangerin creatively adds characters or fleshes out the biblical account of characters, changes events and their order and chronology in order to enable the readers to experience the truth of the story and to feel as well as understand the working of God in their lives. In so doing, Wangerin overcomes much of the distance of culture, time, and lack of detail which many times hinder today's reader from understanding and experiencing the truth of the Biblical stories. And he recognizes as he begins this work that there is one tale "which is no one's imagination, which is true and, therefore, very powerful: the story of Jesus...It is a beautiful tale, a terrible tale, and then again a tale more beautiful than any other." (<u>The Baby Jesus</u>) So in his recounting of the stories from the Bible, Wangerin includes the beautiful stories, the terrible stories, and shows behind all of these stories the hand of God shaping and directing His people through the ages.

As he does in all of his major works, Wangerin tells of the tremendous power of evil, the destructiveness of sin, the forgiveness of God and His final victory over sin and death in the resurrection of Jesus. The symbols he employs are familiar ones to his readers by now: the circles of the world; the silences and the laughter; the destruction of the world because of sin and non-listening; the role of the ideal prophet and/or storyteller in shaping a culture. And these themes and symbols are woven throughout the eight hundred pages of the retelling of Scriptures to enable the reader to truly see the beginning and end of life in God and to make sense of the seemingly random, painful, chaotic events of the present. As Wangerin states in his article "Telling Tales": My stories don't offer doctrines about life and about God; they offer relationship. My stories are the meeting place in which relationships begin, mature, may be experienced whole, may be named, are certainly remembered, live...Religions have existed without theology...But no religion has existed without story...and the story is not story until it is told...Story does not instruct; story makes a cosmos out of chaos...Doctrine may engage the understanding mind, but the story engages the human whole —body, senses, reason, emotion, memory, laughter, tears —so the person who is fragmented is put back together again, and that under governance of a new experience —-the hearing of his own story told."

In a culture which has lost the ability to experience the stories of God in the Christian Bible, Wangerin's work enables his reader to experience God's hand working through the ages in a vital and evocative way. He employs once again all of his well controlled literary techniques and his creativity to bring to life stories that many in our culture have never heard or experienced. A brief discussion of his major symbols and his creative selectivity of the Biblical accounts enables one to understand the scope of this attempt at retelling the Biblical stories of God.

Wangerin by his selectivity of the stories told, his rearranging of the chronology of the events and his creating new characters and events to explain and bring to life obscure events, gives a vital freshness to the Biblical account.Instead of beginning at the creation, Wangerin chooses to begin with the call of Abraham and the promise of the birth of a son to Abraham and Sarah. As the story unfolds, major earlier events are told by other characters, as the characters tell their children of their inheritance, as prophets remind the people of God's covenants, and as parents instruct their children in the stories of their families. Thus, the retelling of the earlier events takes place naturally in the same manner we, today, tell the stories of our families and of God to our children. For example, when David has fled from the anger of Saul, his parents, sisters and brothers are likewise fugitives. When David worries that there is no place to send his parents and family where they will be safe, his Mother tells him to send them to Moab. But David responds, "But Moab is an enemy of Israel!" It then becomes necessary for his mother to tell him the story of Ruth and his background and relationship to Moab:

> "No Son, Moab is an enemy of Saul. Moab is your lineage, my son."

> "What?"
> "There is Moabite blood in your veins."
> "How?"
> Then without moving her old bones, Nahash told David a tale of his inheritance. Long ago there was a famine so severe in Israel that Elimelech of Bethlehem took his wife and his two sons to Moab, to survive there."

At this point in the story, Wangerin retells the Book of Ruth, and the story of David's great-grandmother Ruth. And "David watches his mother tell this story. Ancient, bent, and wrinkled, she took such delight in the remembrance and in the words that her voice had a husky quality. If David had an aptitude for language, he had received it from his Mother."

In another instance, Wangerin has Ezra the priest read the books of the Law to the people of Israel who helped Nehemiah rebuild the wall. Nehemiah meets the priest Ezra and states: "You must read the Book of the Law to this people, he says. "He can't control the urgency in his voice. He glares into the pouchy eyes of the priest. 'Read it word for word. Read it clearly and explain it, so that the people can understand it. They have forgotten Egypt and the Wilderness and Mount Sinai and the Words of God which Moses wrote in the Law. Ezra, priest and scribe, they have forgotten the covenant!"'... So Ezra turns his eyes to see the words in front of him and begins to read. 'In the beginning,' he intones the holy words. 'In the beginning God created the heavens and the earth.'

> 'Ahhh.' Nehemiah sighs to himself; the words.
> Ezra reads with slow articulation. He finds a
> rhythm in the language and slowly, slowly rocks his
> body to the reading: 'In the beginning...'

It is at this point Wangerin tells the beginning of the Scriptures with the story of creation, redemption and sin. And Ezra begins to take on symbolic significance as the true story-teller or priest who is needed by a culture in order for that culture to have shape and meaning. "Suddenly, Nehemiah realizes that Ezra need not read the words in order to know them. The Book of Moses lives whole within him. He sees all the words, and all the laws in a single glance, as from a high mountain. And though the congregation is receiving the story sentence by sentence, for Ezra the priest every sentence contains the entire story from beginning to end." Ezra as true "scop" and storyteller creates a cosmos which enables his hearers to see themselves and their covenant with God more clearly. And Ezra explains to the people what happens when a people forget and break the covenant with God: "What happened at the breaking of the covenant? Life becomes difficult. Work becomes hard. The people who learned to sin against God learn to sin against one another." And as Ezra continues to tell the story of the calling of Noah, the flood, the calling of Abraham, and the rebellion of the children of Israel,

"Suddenly Ezra pauses. there is a sound in the square, very soft, like running water, and for a moment the priest is mystified. But Nehemiah, who is nearer to the people, knows that sound. It is the sound of weeping. The people of Judah are crying...And all of the people continue weeping, releasing ancient griefs, centuries of sorrow." But Ezra tells them not to mourn for this day of the telling of the story is holy to them. So the people do as Ezra tells them to do, and " soon in Jerusalem there is the beginning of consolation, because the people have understood the words that were declared to them." Thus, as in all of Wangerin's works, the telling of truthful story leads to healing and consolation after sin and grief are understood and faced. Countless times, Wangerin puts the words of the Scriptures into the mouths of his characters as they tell the story of God to one another, console one another with it, and help one another understand the chaos of their present world. In the same manner he integrates the Psalms into the mouths of various characters at a time when they help the reader experience the emotions of the Psalms, so that the Psalms are put back into the context of the whole story so that their power to convict, console, and heal can be felt by the reader of Wangerin's work. Thus, when King Saul is disturbed by his nightmares and fits of depression, young David sings his Psalm of despair to Saul:

> O Lord, rebuke me not in fury,
>   Nor chasten me in wrath!
> Thine arrows have found me! Their heads are buried
>   In my heart, point and shaft!
>
> My wounds are foul and festering
>   because of foolishness:
> Oh God, I'm sorry for my sin!
>   My sin., Lord. I confess my sin!
>
> Do not forsake me, O my Lord!
>   Oh, God, Deliver me!
> I wait upon thy kinder word;
>   O Lord, I wait for thee —

Wangerin then uses this repetition of a psalm by David, to give the reader insight into the heart of King Saul: "In the morning Saul could repeat the entire song from memory. He went out of his tent whispering it. The song had become the cry of his heart. It gave expression to the furnace burning within him, and therefore, it gave him comfort.

But suddenly - just as he was reaching for his horse's bridle - the king yelped and whirled around and glared back at the tent. A thought had just pierced him like an arrow, and he understood why David's nighttime presence was so troubling; the man knew too much! With David the king had no secrets! Neither, then, could he maintain a personal privacy with that one - no, nor authority either! David had dared to give expression to the sins of his king! And how ever could he presume to talk about his, Saul's sin?" And from this point Saul's hatred, fear and jealousy of David increase so that he desires to kill him. Many other times Wangerin as the storyteller chooses to put the words of the psalms or of other portions of Scriptures into the mouths of characters that may or may not have originally spoken the words. But each time he does this artistic choice, it is for the purpose of helping the reader understand the ultimate truth and significance of the words. The Song of Solomon is put into the mouth of two female characters: Tamar, the half sister of Solomon and Solomon's wife, the daughter of the pharaoh of Egypt. And by putting these words into the mouths of these characters, the intense longing of the words, and their passionate intensity are juxtaposed as the wife sings of love's fulfillment, and Tamar sings of her unfulfilled love caused by her rape, her loss of her brother and her subsequent widowhood. The development of these two women characters also adds an element of fore-shadowing to the flaws in Solomon's character which will eventually destroy his kingdom. Solomon is seen from the beginning of his kingship as flawed, and although heroic and grand, he is turned into the hero of a Greek tragedy whose fall the reader is prepared for. Those who know him well, especially his Mother Bathsheba warn Solomon and us, the readers of Wangerin's works, of this flaw: "Bathsheba in her sixtieth year was a realist. She knew that there was in this splendid king (Solomon) a flaw that could cost him the kingdom." And later Wangerin writes: "But Bathsheba had stepped away from the festivities. She stood to the side watching her son...The queen mother was alarmed." Later, Bathsheba confronts Solomon with his flaw: "My son, I must in love and good reason speak. No one else will speak as forthrightly as I...I do not fear you...Your weakness. It is not that you make love to many women, but that you let women instruct you, and you obey. God appointed you to decide for Israel. Not your wives...But those whom you love are controlling you!...There are hundreds of women, all wives to you, and everyone of them worships a God who is not our God....But then her son is no longer there. He has departed by the side door into the night."

Likewise the visiting Queen of Sheba asks who was built such an important house, and she hears the caustic reply from the queen mother: "Egypt requests a house of her own, and Israel obeys." Wangerin further reveals Solomon's lack of sensitivity and his flaw through the mind of his sister Tamar at the dedication of the House of God. Tamar is laughing for the joy of her brother when she is carried off, and when she looks, she sees that Solomon is paying no attention to her. The one who carries her off is Benaiah, the murderer of Joab by the order of Solomon, and Tamar states: "I don't like Solomon. He knows nothing of my long sorrow. Widowhood doesn't touch him. Poverty, the scorn of all Jerusalem, the stink of other men's sinning —what does the king know of these things?...I don't like Solomon....But I love him. God help me, I can't stand the torture it causes me." Solomon's grandeur is portrayed by Wangerin as well as his sin and insensitivities and weaknesses, and the reader begins to see a human being in the place of the grand king Solomon. But Wangerin stays true to the story of God even when he changes the events or details, for each change is made to better enable the reader to understand this God who has moved throughout human history and whose story has been told from generation to generation. Sometimes the events are changed or details are added to make God more comprehensible to the reader, and this is the only flaw I see in Wangerin's retelling of the stories, for by changing events and selectively arranging them, he narrows the interpretation to his view and loses some of the powerful ambiguity and incomprehensibleness of God's story. For example, when David is attempting to bring the ark to Jerusalem, and Uzzah reaches out to balance it and is killed, Wangerin doesn't allow that maybe David and his company sinned against God by not bringing the ark back according to the instructions of Moses, but he interprets the reasons taking away the ambiguity and the responsibility:

> As they followed the ark toward Jerusalem
> they moved their feet harder and harder. Uzzah threw
> his arms to heaven and whirled about behind
> the cart. But just as they approached the threshing floor

of Nacon, he slipped on some warm ox droppings
and fell. Uzzah cracked his skull on the stones of
the threshing floor and died instantly.
The word of his death flew backward like an
arrow striking every dancer with mortal terror. They
stood still and whispered, "He must have touched the
Ark! Uzzah defiled the Ark, and the wrath of God has
killed him!"

No one moved. Who knew what God might do
next!"

The king heard the word of the people, and he,
too, grew fearful...

And the elders and all the people of Israel stole
home abashed."

Each time, however, when Wangerin does interpret the text,
he attempts to more closely duplicate the meaning of the original
Hebrew or Greek text and does not compromise his scholarship
to his creativity. Rather, he uses his scholarly knowledge to reveal
to the readers possible new meanings to enable the reader to
expand his/her understanding of the story. He constantly remembers his covenant with his readers to "name seen and unseen reality as truthfully as possible."

Wangerin, like all excellent story tellers, creates the total
truth of the story, and presents a cosmos out of some of the random events of Scripture so that these random events, and the
many unexplainable events in our own lives, are seen in the total
cosmos of God. And the incidences of changing events or adding
detail all fit into the whole telling of the story, and all of the random pieces begin to make sense to the reader. And Wangerin
through his recurring themes and symbols unifies all of the stories of the Bible into a whole artistic work rather than isolated
random stories. And this wholistic approach to the hundreds of
stories of Scripture reveals the cosmos behind the workings of
God throughout human history. By reading Wangerin's works
one can see the "beginning and the end" of human history and
can see the important role of individuals in the fulfilling of God's
ultimate redemption and reconciliation. And it is Wangerin's
elaborate use of symbols and his threading these symbols
throughout The Book of God, that make the work a dynamic, new
story rather than a reparaphrasing of the Scriptures. The symbols
are those that have occurred throughout Wangerin's major works,

and ones which he effectively used, especially in his fictional work, <u>The Crying for a Vision</u>.

The symbols of laughter, and singing, the destruction of the earth by a broken covenant and the silences of God and many of the characters are woven throughout <u>The Book of God</u>. From the laughter of Sarah when she bears Isaac, to the laughter of Shobal at the end of the work, the symbol of laughter integrates the various encounters with God and shows to us the readers the joy that occurs when the Lord touches our lives and fulfills his promises to us. When Sarah gives birth to Isaac fulfilling the long awaited promise of God, Wangerin states: "And before the day was over, Sarah's joy grew too great to be contained. The old woman laughed. She covered her face and laughed soundlessly, so that the entire company fell silent thinking she was crying. But then she rose up and clapped her hands and sang: 'God has made laughter for me! Oh, laugh with me! Let everyone who hears my story laugh! Sisters, sisters, where is your faith? Who guessed yesterday that Sarah would suckle a child today?'...Then Abraham touched her hand and said: 'Old woman, more precious than rubies, we will name the child for laughter. We will name him Isaac.' She was ninety years old. He was one hundred." In the same manner, when God visits the children of Israel and brings them out of Egypt, the children "went forward big-eyed and frightened. Even when dawn began to streak the Eastern sky, people continued grimly, hurrying, hurrying....But...here and there the children heard soft talking. A little early whispering. Then giggling. The young women were giggling. Suddenly a man let out a bark of laughter and immediately shut up. But then another man started to laugh and could not stop. He covered his mouth, but the laughter came out of his nose. His shoulders were shaking. The people who saw him began to grin. Then they chuckled; then they, too, broke into outright laughter. They roared with laughter. They laughed til the tears ran down their cheeks. They covered their stomachs and gasped for air and howled as if they were hurting. Like flocks of wild birds the laughter rose up and flew from family to family, from tribe to tribe throughout the entire congregation of Israel — and this is finally what made the people to stop running from Egypt: laughter. They made the round desert ring with the sound of their joy...So they remembered that the long night of silence had been followed by a day of laughter." One is reminded of the laughter of Miz Lil as she sits with Pastor Wangerin, and the laughter that Wangerin introduces into many of his works as suddenly God breaks through, cosmos and meaning are restored, and the darkness is temporarily forgotten. The laughter breaks out at unlikely places throughout Wangerin's retelling of the stories, and Christ especially is portrayed by Wangerin as a man of laughter. When the woman from Samaria meets Christ after he returns to Samaria one day, Wangerin shows this delightful side of Christ:

> Now, it may be that on the afternoon of her going forth in headlong joy to greet the returning Jesus, one of her small toes hooked a root. Whatever the cause, gladness fled her face. Terror widened her green eyelids. That great woman shrieked: 'Master! Catch me!' Jesus, directly in her orbit, uttered a single astonished bark....He caught her. Or perhaps it is more accurate to say, he broke her fall... Clearly the woman had bruised the master's dignity. But had she also broken some of his bones? No one could tell. He was buried facedown beneath a pile of flesh... The woman initiated attempts to climb off, but then Jesus sucked in an enormous wind and opened his mouth and burst into laughter. He was laughing! He had been laughing already in the dust!...His mouth stretched wide by the ear of the woman, producing wonderful booms of laughter. And when he had turned all the way over, he threw his arms around his massive admirer and hugged her, and she blinked and began to giggle, and he cried, 'Woman, don't love me so much! You could crush me with all your loving!' He released a long fountain of laughter. All his disciples and all of Sychar joined him, roaring at the mountainous love before them. And so it was that the celebration had already begun, laughing, and dancing and the eating of meat."

In the same manner when Peter was asked by Jesus to feed the five thousand, he is overwhelmed until Jesus begins multiplying the fish and loaves. And Wangerin states: "We handed out bread and fish until every man and every woman and every child was satisfied. By nightfall I was grinning. I had a terrible tickling in my stomach, and I would have laughed out loud if everyone else had not been so solemn. He was right! I had been wrong. Against all common sense and reason and facts and reality, the man could fill whole populations of food." Then later, after the disciples depart by boat and Jesus comes walking to them on water, Peter states: "It was Jesus! Walking toward us on the rolling seas! Now I did burst out laughing. Great whoops of laughter —not only that the Lord had come at all, but that he had come in so grand a manner."

Many times Wangerin contrasts the laughter of those who have faith with the tears of those who don't believe God, or the temporary laughter of the wicked with the temporary tears of the righteous, for many times in Wangerin's universe the followers of God are unable to see God's workings and the power of evil seems victorious. But each time the deep laughter of God's children carries through the good news of the stories of God.

Another major image used throughout the work which gives unity and coherence to the many diverse stories is Wangerin's image of the circle which he uses in many earlier works. In the same manner that he employs this symbol in <u>Crying for a Vision</u>, he uses the circles to show completeness and cosmos and sanctuary from chaos. The sanctuary forms the center of the circle of Jewish people, and when the center holds there is celebration. But when the center falls, chaos and meaninglessness take over:

> So the children of Israel pitched camp in that place, according to the instructions of the Lord. The Tabernacle was assembled in the center of two huge circles of tents. Aaron and his people constituted the Eastern side of the circle closest to the Tabernacle — the side to which its door opened. The rest of the inner circle belonged to the families of Levi, so that priests and the servants of the Lord were ever near to serve him. The greater outer ring was composed of the other tribes, so the Lord was in the midst of them all, and Moses bore His word to all the people.

In like manner Wangerin portrays Christ as the center: "So they turned from the road and descended into the Jordan Valley and found him in the very center of activity - like the hub of a great wheel turning. All faces, young and old, yearned toward him. And he was never still. He was never mute." Throughout this work God, his temple, Christ form the center of the universe, and their speech gives it shape and form. But when the characters lose the outward center, they begin to turn in on themselves in circles, and the world no longer makes sense. In the same manner that Fire Thunder turns in on himself and causes the death and suffering of many, so the characters of these stories turn in on themselves: "But Mary was immobile. She could not move...But such shame was running through her limbs that they were paralyzed. 'Oh, Mary, why can't you hold your tongue?'...Mary's head was bowed down, her shoulders rounded; she was circling into herself." Likewise, Judas decides to take everything into his own hands and create his own center apart from Christ. As he states: "Judas had made up his mind. He resolved to accept confusion no more...he could take matters into his own hands and create the clarity that he and the times required." Later Wangerin describes Judas as in a tremendous battle between "cosmic elements, light and darkness, were contending in this poor disciple's soul." By the end of this story of God that Wangerin writes, the two symbols are brought together after the resurrection of Christ:

> As the stories of the Lord's appearing spread, so did remembrance of his teaching — and so did joy.
>
> Shobal, whose name means Basket, the odd fellow out of whom Jesus had cast an evil spirit, suddenly walked into the upper room and started to laugh. A drooling, lank sort of laughter. He tried to stop, but he couldn't. He laughed and laughed, and the first one to laugh with him was Mary the mother of Jesus, who had not laughed in many a year. Mary and Shobal laughed like children together, holding hands and turning circles. And most of the disciples became infected with the dithering joy. They barked and bellowed and giggled and roared.

Laughter, circles, childlikeness, all images permeating Wangerin's works as cosmos is restored; meaning is restored; joy is restored. And throughout is always the idea of the storyteller, the scop who makes sense of reality and tells the story to others. And the concept of the true story, which enables one to glimpse meaning and purpose and truth, fills this latest work of Wangerin's. And as he states in the Epilogue: the story was told over and over throughout the Bible and has continued to be told for the last two thousand years since the completion of the Christian written Bible.

All of Wangerin's storytelling ability and his mature literary style contribute to the wholeness and power of this work. His tremendous focusing on small details to involve the readers; his creation of strange but memorable characters who interact with God and with each other; his intimate description of distinguishing characteristics of each of the Biblical characters; and his creative and joyful use of words —all combine to add to the quality of his work. Although he adheres to the Biblical text for the majority of his stories, his addition of new characters, his creation and/or clarification of human relationships; and his adding of details cause the events to lose their distance from the reader. Probably one of the most graphic examples of these additions and their effectiveness in involving the reader occurs with the characterization of Achan. Although the Bible tells of his destruction because of his hoarding of spoil from the battle, Wangerin creates a whole world of family and relationships around him. His mother and father, Carmi and Elisheba are introduced as she gives birth to Achan during the crossing of the Red Sea, so that he is the first born after the flight from Egypt. As she thirsts and hungers during the journey, the reader sympathizes with the plight of this young mother and the frustration of her husband at being unable to provide for her and his son. Then as Carmi complains and dreams, the reader is involved in the harshness of the journey. Carmi is the one Wangerin uses to make real to the reader the disobedience to God in the gathering of too much manna, the complaining because of thirst or the lack of meat, the mumbling against God and Aaron. As Wangerin describes him: "Carmi, however, was a man of extremes. He was worried for his baby and brought home six omers. During the day they ate three. That night he congratulated himself on having provided for the next day, but by dawn his store was stinking and crawling with worms."... "With the added swagger of self-righteousness, they complained loudly in public places. Carmi was among the loudest...and he yells at Moses, 'Moses, do you hear me? I am the voice of ten thousand now. I am pointing at a jar of manna! I am remembering manna, day after day for thirty years, manna! And I gag! I say for ten thousand, we loathe this worthless food!' That same night Carmi the son of Zabdi died. He was bitten by a snake...and the man chose silence at the end...Once he opened his eyes and looked up at his wife. His countenance seemed to say, I expected nothing else. And then he breathed his last." Wangerin describes his wife as also being bitten by a snake, but Achan carries his mother to a place where she can look upon the snake erected by Moses and live. But later this same Achan, who has learned so much about greed and self-centeredness from his father steals the treasures of Jericho..."Forty years old. He had been the firstborn of the new generation, for his mother delivered him even as Israel was passing through the sea from Egypt into freedom. Achan. The son of his mother, Elisheba faithful soul who died at their second crossing, from the wilderness over the Jordan into the land of promise...They dug into Achan's tent and brought out the things that had been devoted to destruction....And they burned all that Achan was: his oxen, his asses, his sheep, his tent, his possessions, his sons, his daughters, his wife, and himself. They burned him with fire, and they stoned him with stones, and he was no more, and Carmi's heritage passed from the earth...Thereafter, the name of that place was called Valley of Trouble."

So many wonderful images are created in this work that only a few can be mentioned to illustrate the descriptive detail of this author; for example, the last image of the king of Jericho as the walls collapse: "And the final vision vouchsafed unto the king was a piece of wall which neither crumbled or burned, a slim finger of stone with one window two stories up, from which hung a scarlet cord. In the last instant of his life the world seemed to the king a bitter joke — for why should that one live and not another? The window belonged to an outcast! A whore named Rahab!" Or the image of the mother of Barabbas begging for the life of her son, and Jesus' recognition of her love for her son and his admiration of her; or the image of the little girl whose parents are killed, and she is maimed when Barabbas is captured, and Longinus' searching for her after the crucifixion to raise her as his own. Wangerin creates concrete detail after concrete detail to bring to life the many movements of God through the story of the Bible. He consistently gives motivations for an individual's actions and traces the consequences of these actions through the narrative as they are confronted with truth and either believe it or reject it.

As usual Wangerin is the master of the craft of writing, carefully choosing words, contrasting short and long sentences to bring attention to an event, using one sentence paragraphs to emphasize a point. And the reader is immediately drawn into the characters, the artistic distance is removed and the distances that the Bible many times imposes caused by the alien culture, the enormous span of time, or the lack of detail in the Biblical accounts are eliminated by Wangerin's artistry.

Wangerin encourages his readers to "pay attention" to the smallest details of the Biblical story and of their own lives, and to realize that God is working throughout cultures and within individuals to bring knowledge of himself to the world. As he does in The Crying for a Vision Wangerin quickly brings the work to an end after the perfect sacrifice has been offered, for at that point order has been restored, chaos has been defeated, and the story just needs to be retold from generation to generation to change people and form the center of their world. So Andrew, the shy disciple, overcomes his shyness and tells the story, Peter, the blundering, denying disciple is forgiven and given a mission, Mary the mother of Jesus is dancing in a circle with Shobal, and Mary Magdalene overcomes her self-depreciation and becomes a part of God's family. Even the thief on the cross, who turns out to be the son of the bleeding woman whom Christ healed, is forgiven, and Longinus, the Roman soldier who arrested Barabbas, helped crucify Christ, and helped Joseph of Arimathea take him from the cross is left pondering the confusion of his life. "The Sabbath arrived. But Longinus did not observe it. He was not a Jew. Neither was he the Roman he had been. The events of that day inaugurated for him a time of crippling confusion. He left the army completely, seeking no reward at his departure...And then he went through Jerusalem seeking a small child whose hands had been disfigured by burning half a year ago...Therefore, the Roman decided that if she had been abandoned, he would raise her as his own. If, on the other hand, her uncle loved her and was caring for her after all, then Longinus would offer his help as a brother to Barabbas, a second uncle to the niece. And if that were not acceptable, then he would be a servant to them both." And we see the two disciples on the road to Emmaus, Cleopus and his daughter, visited by Christ and filled with joy. And the story that Wangerin has told in this work has been told "in countless languages and innumerable are the hearts that have been shaped by it."

This work is truly the work of a mature story teller whose literary and artistic talents are brought together to weave a powerful story of God and his intervention in the lives of humans.

Chapter XI.

WANGERIN'S COVENANT
WITH THE READER

WANGERIN'S COVENANT
WITH THE READER

"It has ever been my notion that the writer by writing is asking for companionship, and the reader by reading is responding 'Yes.'

Then each book written becomes at its reading a covenant for a while:

Walk with me.
Words are the touch between us.

And the Word Himself is the life and the
light and the grace of any such
friendship - ever."

Walter Wangerin, Jr., takes his writing very seriously and refuses to compromise his artistic vision, and he faithfully reveals to his reader the true seeing of his soul. He observes life carefully and minutely but remains childlike in his reactions to it -- extremely aware of reality but listening carefully to the harmony beyond the chaos, sensing the beauty beneath the surface ugliness. As he expresses in his portrayal of the birth of Jesus: "that which the camera could record of Jesus does not inspire awe...If, for us, reality is material only, data, documentation: if truth for us is merely empirical, then we are left with a photograph of small significance....No, I choose to stay a child. My picture shall not be undimensioned, therefore, neither as flat as a photograph nor as cold as a news copy - no never as cold as a scientist's case study." ("Painting Christmas")

In all of his works, fictional and nonfictional, his drawings of life are many layered; he never renders reality only, but multi-dimensional reality always revealing the center which holds the world together. Behind his precise and accurate descriptions of character and realities, "in the perfect center of all his circles and of all the spheres of the world...there is the center of everything; there, himself, the center that holds all orbits in one grand and universal dance is Jesus."

But Wangerin never allows his religious convictions to become moralistic and preachy, rather he is a writer who is a Christian, and, therefore, one whose works, because they reflect the inner truth of that vision resemble the Christian world and the Christian ideas. But he allows his stories to stand on their own artistic wholeness rather than interpreting them for the reader. This ability to tell truthful stories without degenerating to shallow moralism or surface preachiness requires that he carefully empathizes with the people around him and then that he with creativity and integrity portrays these human encounters with a kind of "watchful serendipity" always aware of the possible value or potential epiphany within even the smallest event. Although his works are seldom strictly autobiographical, because they are so intimately linked to his daily observation and perception of life, they are truly his own unique stories. As Jill Baumgartner states: "His continuing narration is bound up in his past and his individuals can never be separated from tradition." Wangerin begins Miz Lil with the cautionary statement: "The stories in this book are true. They happened. But I've made the aesthetic and ethical decision sometimes to conflate events...and sometimes to invent the detail and the character which the deeper spirit of the story required. In this manner I've tightened the pace of human life considerably." One of Wangerin's major talents as an artist is to select only those events which do illuminate the truth and deeper spirit of his stories, and his fictions are quick-moving and intense because of this tightening of the pace of human life. As Chekhov stated: "Any fool can write. It takes a genius to erase." Wangerin knows how to erase the non-essential from his works so that the reader doesn't get bogged down and, thus, miss the deeper truths presented.

Wangerin can be trusted as an artist because he believes that art cannot exist apart from community, and the communal covenant he makes with his readers is very important to him for he knows the power of words both to bring forth truth and to create lies. Wangerin briefly outlines four covenants that he has committed himself to as a writer:

1. Covenant of Reality - Wangerin believes that his art needs to draw truthfully and carefully from observed reality. As one can see from all of his works, Wangerin deeply observes reality and accurately describes and reflects this world in which the reader lives. Without this interactive involvement with and observation of external life, Wangerin believes that his works would distance themselves or alienate themselves from the reader.

2. Covenant of Craft - Wangerin has carefully learned his craft and how to use these techniques of writing effectively. Without these skills, his works would not be aesthetically pleasing nor precise in their usage of language. Thus, Wangerin has committed himself to learning his craft well so that the technique or lack thereof never interferes with the truth of the story. As he states in "A Review of Today's Good Writing and Good Writers":

> "You cannot take it for granted that just because an author has chosen to write about things that we consider true and essential and trenchant, this author also writes well. A devout person is not necessarily a good writer. Books faithful to certain principles of doctrine may be wretchedly faithless to principles of good literature. Much, much of 'religious' material published today is ignorant of the power, the variety, the grace, the flexibility, the color, precision, and holy vitality of the very medium in which it is published. It doesn't know language. It doesn't know what prose can do. It doesn't know art....The truth is affected by the form in which it is presented. Cheap language will make the message seem cheap. Shoddy prose presents a slipshod truth."

But Wangerin also realizes that the skill to use language well requires an ethical decision on the part of the writer not to misuse it for untruth, propaganda or manipulation. Wangerin knows that explosive creativity can destroy others, can tell lies and get people to believe these lies. And he strongly believes that "There are some things you do not do, not because you cannot do them, but because you should not....The technical mastery of an author may excite our admiration but a good writer is not necessarily a writer of goodness...Effective art is a subtle, pervasive persuader. It teaches the people how to 'see' by giving them sight and insight in an intense, controlled experience. Willy nilly art affects the reader's sense of the Truth. Beautiful emptiness, then, can be subversive for persuading the votive reader of emptiness.

"Meaning Matters!

"Meaning matters in art, for the very solace and security and spiritual health of an age, however secular it boasts itself..." ("A Review of Today's Good Writers and Good Writing," p. 4)

This integrity found in Wangerin's art is unusual in our mass consumption culture in which it is so easy for the artist to lie and to profit from the people's naiveté and willingness to be entertained only or from their satisfaction with lies or half truths.

3. Covenant of Audience - Wangerin in his works attempts to portray reality accurately but also attempts to name rightly and correctly. To peer beneath the surface of reality and to lie about what is seen or to misname it hurts the reader and is bad art. To manipulate his words in order to create a cosmos in his works, but to ignore the truths of this world and the underlying myth of it would also be bad art and a distortion of reality according to Wangerin. This doesn't mean that he doesn't take risks in his works, but he will not deceive his reader. Although individual characters in his works may misname or falsely name reality, Wangerin's stories are always true to his vision of reality and can be trusted. Thus, he doesn't ignore evil or gloss over death or not draw attention to the self-centeredness of the world -- but he also doesn't ignore sacrifice, grace, beauty, love, and the ultimate signifying by God.

4. Covenant of Faith - Because of Wangerin's unique vision of truth, he always in his works reflects the world of faith, but he also covenants not to preach at the reader. He never explains his faith in his works, but the Christian faith forms the backdrop against which the characters interact. His works create a cosmos of faith through which the reader can see the order behind the chaos. And many times the faith is not named but is just deeply entrenched in the world of the story.

As stated earlier Wangerin believes that as a writer his job is to take this amorphous and chaotic world which many times seems to be falling apart and to give it shape. To sing the particular events, the absurd happenings of life and to compose these events in such a way that the reader can begin to hear the harmony behind the disharmony of life. The artist, according to Wangerin, does not create a new order or a new world; he composes the events of everyday life in such a way that the old truths and order of the universe are no longer lost on the reader but are woven into the daily events. Art may name reality using different names but these names are truthful and revealing.

Wangerin is very aware of his artistic vision and of the power of the story to stand on its own without interpretation. As he states, "My story does not instruct in definitional, doctrinal meanings...but by its very ambiguity it does something better than that: story makes a cosmos out of chaos...many times story undefines; it is like a lightning bolt in the midst of a herd." His stories may shake the reader from complacency and common perceptions in order to prepare the reader for a deeper truth. Because of this unsettling aspect of his writings, "his stories are dangerous and ambiguous." They confront the reader wholistically with the signifying truth of God, and may change the reader's perceptions of reality even after the cosmos of the story is left behind.

His stories are times of "encounter - moments of intensest interaction...they are significant; they testify each time they are told to the timeless relationship with the Deity. But my stories are also signifying - that is they make sense of the experiences which people suffer in the present, the common stuff of their lives; they are signs which name and contain a storm of immediate feelings, helpless impulses, shifting human relationships, spiritual yearnings: in this way people are relieved of confusion."

One is reminded as one reads and listens to Wangerin of Fools Crow's concept of oral storytelling in the Lacota tradition: "The storyteller is he who takes it upon himself to speak formally...He assumes responsibility for his words, for what is created at the level of his human voice...He realizes the power and beauty of language and the power of words and is careful to use them with precision." (Lacota Storytelling, p. 154)

The precision with which Wangerin uses words is seen in how carefully he chooses his words, so that each word implies, explains or limits the next. This precision of word choice is clearly seen when one looks closely at Wangerin's work, The Crying for a Vision. To describe Fire Thunder, the one who brings so much suffering upon the Lacota people, he states: "This was his custom, to stay at the edge of circles. He wore no adornment. He never put himself forward. He never had....Emotionless, cold, solitary even in a crowd, Fire Thunder lived at the edge of circles." In contrast to Fire Thunder, Waskn Mani (Moves Walking) felt so happy to "be in the center of all these circles; the fires first; then the people whose sweat and sage gave him comfort and whose laughter he loved with his whole heart; next the circle of tipis like silent guards around them; then trees of the forest, murmuring, nodding at the tops of them; and then forever and ever the plains, the Earth. The sky. All." As the novel continues, one realizes what happens when all of the sacred circles are broken, and the center no longer holds. Fire Thunder's presence always interrupts the sacred circles of life. When the people are preparing to catch the waga chan (sacred cottonwood tree) - that sacred tree which must never touch the ground, which first they would catch and carry it down into the dance circle, Fire Thunder arrives. "So when the cottonwood cracked from his stump and came tearing down through the canopy of the forest, many men below were caught by surprise. They sprang back in terror, fearing to be crushed. Those left behind were too few to catch the giant and waga chan hit the ground." Wangerin's sparse and exact descriptions prepare the reader for the major conflict of the novel as the sacred circle of life is broken, the sacred circles of the Lacota are disrupted, and one man, powerful and a leader, and one small boy, small and powerless, are forced to confront each other to save the Lacota from total chaos and destruction.

Wangerin uses his language so sparingly and effectively that his works, especially his longer ones, always produce a sense of form and beauty to the reader as they flow effortlessly to present a finished surface. He carefully disentangles the significant from the random, meaningless or irrelevant, and his symbols grow organically and unforced from his stories. In The Crying for a Vision the fires, circles, stars, scorched woman mountain, water lilies - all are interwoven to add depth and layers of meaning to a very simple retelling of the Lacota myths. Wangerin's comments in his Introduction to this work reflect the seriousness with which he writes: "For although it is fiction, I've woven Indian legends into my tale, sometimes whole, sometimes just the threads, taking the tone and the vision of a legend but making the narrative new. For I spent many years studying this culture at its strongest, proudest period - when it was still untroubled by the intrusions of the Wasidrus - and have sought to commemorate the glory by reproducing its history and tradition as accurately as possible." But this retelling is not to record a history but to show forth the universal element within the Lacota which reveal the deeper truths of human life. "For my story presents the Lacota as oyate icke indeed, that common people in whom all peoples might see themselves. Therefore, good and evil mix in them just as virtue and vice exist together in any one family or nation on earth.

"For I have found in the Lacota vision a rich analogue for the relationship any people of genuine faith experience with creation and the Creator. It was my fortune, then -- and my artistic choice -- to use their world as the controlling metaphor of this novel."

> "Reader, wachin ksapa yo! Look not at the tale
> but through it for the truth."

Just as Wangerin is attentive to the world around him, for he knows that in the smallest detail or most unseemly moment he may understand truth, so he urges his readers to be attentive to all of his stories and to look through them for the truth. Because Wangerin studies life carefully and then artistically chooses episodes through which deeper truth can be seen, he is able to keep an emotional distance from his characters, even when he is telling of his own failures and childhood. His works are intense and very personal but not self-conscious; the artist in Wangerin's most effective works disappears from the work in favor of the narrator who is a created fictional character even when speaking of events in the artist's own life. Wangerin, like Madelaine L'Engle, knows "complete dependence on listening to the story and trying to set it down faithfully." (Story that is Higher) In other words, his moral doesn't control the story, and he subordinates everything to the moral; the story controls and unfolds from within and the deeper truth is evoked. And this deeper truth is revealed through human relations, and these relationships are a dominant part of his fiction.

For as he asks in Mourning into Dancing: "Where is there life and not relationship?

"Nowhere. No, Not anywhere in all the grand cosmos of God. And God saw all that he had made and, behold it was good....Good was the first interaction of all things, nothing separated from another thing. Good was the harmony of the cosmos. And very good the life experienced therein, the life sustained by an unbroken network of countless relationships. This wholeness was the intent of the Creator, the perfect will of God and perfect life for us."

Most of the conflicts in Wangerin's novels and short stories describe the breaking of these relationships and then the moments that bring their healing. This break can occur with humans' relationship with God, with creation, with others and with themselves...And love is the very stuff of relationship. Death of relationship and recognition of this death are necessary before healing can begin, so through the portraying of relationships in his works, Wangerin enables us as readers to see ourselves and our relationships more wholly and to be healed. Thus, at the end of each of his writings, relationships are restored, nature is renewed, forgiveness is received, and hope and love are recognized once again.

As Pertelote sings at the end of The Book of Sorrows, "the grey Wolf Chinook leaves the form of Boreas and comes to Pertelote and bowed her head and listened, and then there were two women together to make a common memory of the ones they loved...And far, far away the Brothers Mice pulled their noses from the circle in which they slept...and Chalcedony the crippled Hen touched the fawn to wake her." And in The Crying for a Vision, Fire Thunder is gazing down on the infant in his arms. "With a tremendously huge thumb he brushes snowflakes from her cheek. Immediately she twists her face around to find that thumb with her mouth, then she sighs and settles to sucking. She finds Fire Thunder's good eye and looks at it." In Miz Lil, suddenly "her hand is on the Pastor's knee. 'Pastor, why are you crying?' And so suddenly the truth slips from me: 'Because you're talking with me.'" Even in the death of a loved one, Wangerin has the relationship renewed and continuing as shown in "The Spittin' Image." "And my mother, whether she knew it or not, had said no less. I did more than look like Grandpa Stork. His Spirit, his character and force of his being dwelt within me. When I put forth my boyhood hand to touch her, why, it was as well the hand of her Father. Her Father had come consoling her, not gone at all, not altogether gone, abiding in his grandson, one.'"

In all of his stories the underlying truth is that our relations to each other, to ourselves, and to nature reflect the wholeness or brokenness of our relationship to God, and many times it is through our relationships with others that we grow the most and hear the voice of God. "Perhaps it is people to people that we experience life most immediately, continually and intensely. If the relationship with God is life for us, then the complex network of relationships with other humans completes the human life: the potential God breathes into us becomes a human communion, actual. Here we come to know ourselves. Here, in the deepest sense, we realize our lives...but life is vulnerable. Relationships break."

And this breaking and vulnerability become the major elements in Wangerin's fictional works. And when our human relationships reveal us to ourselves and enable us to reach out in love to one another, then to God, then "our natural relationships can honor the earth with wisdom and care, can bless and serve the creation God put into our hands for safe-keeping...And our internal relationships become both truthful and unembarrassed." (Mourning into Dancing)

Wangerin is brutally honest in his works, revealing human failures and shortcomings, but part of his honesty is based on the healing of the internal relationships in his works. His characters learn that in spite of the hurts they have caused, they are loved and forgiven, not only by the others with whom they have a relationship but by God as well: "You can be more honest if you know that you are forgiven. If you are scared that you are not forgiven, you don't tell anyone anything. If you are forgiven, you can be more honest about the sin that is over." ("Inner City Ministry") So Wangerin honestly portrays his characters and their shortcomings and his own failures and shortcomings in his more personal stories. "Anytime I write, or tell stories on myself, and refer to my sinfulness or my foolishness, it's not a story which is not over. It's not a story that's in the middle. It's a story that is done. The completion was in forgiveness."

Forgiveness, hope even in death and suffering, love and healed relationships, these form the optimism of Wangerin's realistic fictions. And the good he portrays in his work is always more powerful than the darkness and evil he portrays. His stories weave a world, like the stories of Hans Christian Andersen did for him as a child, a world which "genuinely acknowledges all the monsters in us...that is honest about evil and the tendency to evil in each of us. And he offers us hope in his tales for even when evil has been chosen, forgiveness may follow -- therein lies extraordinary hope...Never, never does Andersen compromise the truth of human experience for children's ears," and never does Wangerin compromise the power of evil for his reader -- but also never does he weaken the good and hope. As the stories of Andersen were read to Wangerin as a child, Wangerin states: "Night after night my Father read the stories...Night after night I live the adventures that order my turbulent days and shape my waking self, my instincts, my faith, my adulthood to come. Optimism grows in me and hope in the midst of suffering, and this third thing too, perhaps the most difficult of all - forgiveness for my own most self- centered and wretched sins. Not the doctrine of forgiveness. Not the concept. Forgiveness in fact, as a mold to my experience ever hereafter. Andersen's world is a dramatic enactment of theologies which the child simply cannot grasp in the abstract." ("Shaping the Child")

So in Wangerin's tales, we the readers experience forgiveness, love and hope even in the midst of the honest portrayal of sin, hurts, suffering and death. And Wangerin is not teaching these to us so that we learn them intellectually; he shows them forth so that the experience of his characters becomes our experience, the forgiveness offered becomes our forgiveness, the hope becomes our hope, and we experience the highest truths of our faith. And when Orpheus prays at the end in perfect peace "quietly, straight into the ear of Jesus," so we the reader experience the closeness and forgiveness of God. And when Pertelote sings Compline at the end of The Book of Sorrows, she sings it for the reader, and each of us "lifts our heads from sleep and looks at the sky and sees the stars, and these become the blanket for our bed, and we resolve never to forget the song nor the singer." We can face the monsters, chaos and evil in our lives with hope because we have not "learned but experienced the highest truths of our faith. Not in doctrine but in fact..." Just as Wangerin's Father gave him the gift of faith so that he can face death, his Father's and others, so Wangerin through his works gives his readers the ability "to act in liberty, free from the need to lie, free from fear...able to face evil and death with hope and with clear eyes, undeceived and undenying."

Chapter XII.

NON-FICTIONAL WORKS

NON-FICTIONAL WORKS

"I intend this book to be both practical and personal as though I were your Pastor, and we sat discussing holy, intimate necessities over a cup of cof-
fee. I'll seek to find you and define your experience
by offering myself, my knowledge, my faith, and my
own experience."

Wangerin introduces Chapter Two of his work <u>As for Me and
My House</u> with the above quote, but it could well introduce all of
his non-fictional works. His honesty, skill with words, ability to
find significance in daily encounters and to see the workings of
God behind them, all make his non-fictional works as valued and
unique as his fictional writings. His works all discuss deep truths
using personal experiences of himself and others as the vehicle
for revealing the significance of these truths to our daily lives. As
he states at the end of <u>Mourning into Dancing</u>:

"'Gloria...I've written a book about you. Is that
OK? A book. I'm really telling a difficult story, which
can be good for all people...I'm describing the time of
his dying and the time that came afterward - especially the feelings...all of them....Some of the feelings
were hard and bad. Some were downright horrible.
Some were good. I'm telling all of them.'

"She said quietly, 'Why?...Why tell my feelings?'

"'Because it's through our feelings that God
works to change things. Because you had to have
those feelings even to know how close God was to

155

you...But you survived...Even by those feelings, Gloria, God raised you up again.'

"With her eyes still closed she said, 'But why do you have to tell them out loud? In a book?'

"'For anyone who doesn't know what you know,' I said. 'Especially for the people I love. For Talitha -- who thinks she knows everything; but who is going to be humbled, as you say. No one can keep death away; and so many people don't know that. Well, and then they don't know the goodness of the hard feelings...but you do.'"

So all of his works and the stories intertwined into his discussions are for those who haven't experienced all of the feelings and a deeper understanding of the main issues of our lives and of our faith: death and suffering, grief, marriage, child-parent relationships, aging parents, ministry and God's workings in our lives and others -- each of these issues Wangerin sensitively discusses in his works with "sharp, surprising insights." Wangerin's works do not explain or reduce mysteries to rational thinking or attempt to give simplistic answers (or in many cases any answers) to complex questions, but they do honestly face the human condition with its joys and sorrows, unions and separations, love and self-centeredness, life and death, and they see the center around which all of these revolve (which is in Christ) and enable the reader to see the significance of the workings of God in each moment. As he explains in his article "Painting Christmas": "But then here, in the perfect center of all my circles and of all the spheres of the world; here is the center of all the galaxies; in the center of thought and love and human gesture, blazing with light more lovely than sunlight -- here, I say, in the center of everything, brightening all things even to the extremes of time and eternity -- here, himself, the center that holds all orbits in one grand and universal dance is Jesus!" And all of these works of Wangerin's keep pointing to the possibilities of hope in the midst of the worst tragedies of life because Christ is the center.

And since Wangerin holds that "Truth may be proffered like pennies in doctrines, but Holy Truth, the core force, the motive and goal of any religion, is a living thing and desires relationship with the people who seek relationship with it, he tells stories for story is the meeting place in which relationships begin, mature, may be experienced whole, may be named, are certainly remembered, lived. In all of his non-fiction, stories are intermingled throughout. Stories of his own childhood, the experiences of his children, his parish members, his family members -- stories which illustrate and make whole the theological and psychological truths being offered. And in these works many times it is the story which was meant as mere illustration, "that so overwhelms its thesis that it comes to life...and works its own wondrous blessings on the reader apart from the explanations." Thus these works "invite the reader to their world,"and these works and the stories they contain become "signifying: that is they make sense of the experiences which people suffer in the present, the common stuff of their lives." And by reading these writings of Wangerin people can be comforted "not as though their lives were explained to them intellectually and they understood (though that understanding does occur on one level), but rather as though a loving and powerful parent came and put arms around them, and they were comforted." ("Telling Tales")

Because of the personal, honest, and narrative way Wangerin writes these longer non-fictional works, Bob Hudson in his forward to <u>Little Lamb Who Made Thee</u> states: "The stories in this book prepared my soul for parenthood in a way that no self-help book could ever have done. It vitalized my understanding of what it means to be a child, a parent, and both at the same time. Yet the book's value is not just in its many wonderful insights into parenthood, or its rollicking humor or in the author's warm and sometimes painful memories of childhood. No, this book is important because on a deep level it isn't really about children and parents at all....It's about maturity - spiritual maturity - at all ages, a process that starts in childhood and should still be continuing when we enter...that city brighter than the sunlight." All of his works ultimately transcend their titles and are about spiritual maturity, becoming like "little children" in God's kingdom, keeping our sense of awe and wonder and hope and belief into adulthood. And Wangerin because he refuses to accept the narrow sophistications of a "realistic" world, composes a theological world, not of narrow doctrines and definitions, but of relationships, and wonder, and finding God in small events, and resurrection. Wangerin believes, like Madelaine L'Engle expresses so well, "That when we are truly remembering, suddenly the mighty acts of God are present. And then we are in kairos. Kairos. God's time....My heart lifts at the first great cry which brought creation into being: Christ...It's the Word, the Light coming to us as Jesus of Nazareth, which confounds my imagination....Most of the time the fact that it is impossible (to my rational mind) doesn't bother me. I live by the impossible....The only God who seems to me to be worth believing in is impossible for humans to understand....I sense a wish in professional religious mongers to make God possible, to make him comprehensible to the naked intellect, domesticate him so that he's easy to believe in...But a comprehensible God is no more than an idol...I don't want that kind of God." (L'Engle, The Irrational Season, p. 19)

Wangerin refuses to reduce the mystery of God's working in this world and through relationships to an intellectually comprehensible and easily categorized theology. As he explains: "If, for us, reality is material only; if we gaze at (Christ's) birth with that modern eye which acknowledges nothing spiritual, sees nothing divine, demands the hard facts only, data, documentation; if truth for us is merely empirical then...we must ourselves live lives bereft of meaning: nothing spiritual, nothing divine, no awe, never a gasp of adoration, never the sense of personal humiliation before glory nor the shock of personal excitation when Glory chooses to...love....Our seeing reveals our soul....No, I will not accept the narrow sophistications and dead-eyed adulthoods of a realistic world. I choose to stay a child. My picture shall not be undimensional...I will paint with baby awe, wide-eyed...And I will call it true; for it sees what is but is not seen. It makes the invisible obvious." ("Painting Christmas")

Wangerin's non-fictional works (as well as all of his fictional works) are invaluable to the reader who desires truth, signifying truth, rather than facts and accurate case studies and reporting. And it is Wangerin's unique sensitivity to the movements of God in the ordering of the events of life and his ability to relate these "intensest moments of encounter with the Deity"in precise, clear and honest prose that make his works different from many Christian writers. "It's a matter of sensitivity. What makes Walter Wangerin, Jr. such a wonderful guide of the Spirit is that he is so articulate in describing our common lifelong struggle to be more aware of God, to open ourselves to his love and presence...Sensitivity and wonder, finally, find their common ground in humility...Walter Wangerin, Jr. as an adult writer is 'full of wonder, quick to sense the mysteries of God's Spirit, open to wonder and to humble convictions of sin.'" (Intro.: <u>Little Lamb Who Made Thee</u>)

Wangerin's first book-length work, <u>As for Me and My House: Crafting Your Marriage to Last</u>, is not a typical self-help, easy solution marriage manual. In fact, its honesty and its portrayal of the sin, self-centeredness, and hurts that can easily destroy the love and spontaneity of a marriage relationship make one realize how carefully the marriage relationship has to be tended if it is to grow and mature. Wangerin refuses to define roles, play games with labeling of male and female traits, and lays the blame for most failures on self-centeredness, insensitivity to another's need, and spiritual immaturity. He means for the book to be practical, setting forth the labor required of a marriage couple and the rewards of that labor. Much of this is accomplished by the author's retelling of his own misconceptions about marriage, mistakes and selfishness, and how he and his wife overcame the obstacles that are sure to confront each marriage. "So the recently married couple has a job to do, a good job, a hopeful and rewarding job, but labor nevertheless. And it will take a patient, gentle energy to accomplish this labor well....At the beginning, I pray that you understand that crisis is common to all couples! No couple needs to fear, in the first year of marriage, that they've made a mistake; that they are 'in trouble,' or that their particular experience is unique. Simply, they have work to do, and God has prepared them to do it...This is the work of accommodation and self-adjustment." From this pragmatic beginning Wangerin develops his thesis discussing such practical themes as the kind of relationship marriage is to be; what forgiveness is; how to practice forgiveness; sharing the work of survival; making love; helping one another; and gifting and volunteering.

Wangerin intermixes with his honest and compassionate dialog events from his own marriage from which he and his wife have learned wisdom and love. And his retelling of these emotional interactions in their own marriage easily enables the reader to be drawn into the narrative and to identify with the labor - "hopeful labor that is marriage." As Bill and Gloria Gaither stated: "Warm and vulnerable, his <u>As For Me and My House</u> is shot throughout with poignant truth and disarming honesty. Walter is not an aloof professional...he is a husband, a lover, sometimes a sinner, who lives with us through the pain and the glory of life's most intimate relationships and gives us all the courage to make grace and forgiveness as much a part of our house as mash potatoes and four-poster beds."

Like his fictional works, Wangerin's non-fictional works are honest, aware of small nuances that make or destroy a relationship, and on the surface his works seem simple and straight forward to read, but one soon realizes that they are deep in their implications and spiritual maturity. He doesn't gloss over the pain, self-centeredness, critical spirit and disillusionment involved in learning to live with another person, nor does he suggest easy solutions - mature, sometimes simple solutions, but not easy. For example, as he discusses the beginning of a marriage relationship he states bluntly: "Idealization will surely run upon realization. Visions shatter on the rock of fact. The question is not how one might avoid this crisis because we can't. It will occur. The question, rather is, what work is required to meet the crisis and to grow by it? For if we think that this revelation of the real spouse is the final truth of our mate and of our marriage -- and that we've made a dreadful mistake, therefore -- then we will move to alienation, one from the other. But if we take this as a natural step in the process of growing one together, we may with clear sight, move toward acceptance and accommodation....When the realization comes, instead of withdrawing in anxiety or blame, praise the Lord, and call it opportunity."

One of the strengths in Wangerin's thinking is that all growth whether in our relationship to God, in ourselves, or to another person, requires change for "relationship is ever and ever a dramatic thing, subsisting not in definitions which freeze it to objectify it, but in the changing itself. The changing is the livelihood of relationship," even though change many times is painful. So marriage is a constant changing and growth process, never static unless we allow it to become so and then we kill the relationship. Marriage like faith is a verb and is in constant flow, and this flowing and changing keeps the relationship from becoming stagnant and to "be in marriage is ever to be moving through the passages of marriage and to be moved by them." "For if the two," he states, "had remarried in a pre-nuptial dream world, your marriage could not work in this in-factual, demanding world. You did not, after all, marry a fiction. You married a person, beloved of God, imperfect indeed, but substantial, real, and vital...Dream-wives and dream-husbands would abhor your own imperfections and vanish before your fleshly humanity. But this real spouse of yours can accept

160

and accommodate herself, himself, to the real you."

But this changing and growth will cause pain because "sin, the arrogant, personal drive to godlikeness in authority and solitary self-importance, has so snarled the marital bond that, though we will always desire to live with another human, yet living together causes pain. We will want it: but it will hurt us. We may produce a good - marvelous good in marrying (just as a woman brings forth a marvelous baby), but we will produce it through tribulation and labor." But since growth is necessary for healthy marriages, Wangerin encourages the reader to go through the many stages of growth constantly enabling the reader to see and feel the necessary steps by his use of stories and personal histories. He first outlines the ideal relationship of marriage, the destructiveness of sin, then the necessity of forgiveness, with practical suggestions of what forgiveness truly means and how we can be empowered to forgive because of our forgiveness from God. All of his discussions center on grace in marriage as opposed to the law of marriage - the new covenant in marriage. "Grace -- this displaces the marriage contract again and again with newness. And this images in action the divine face of the Lord Jesus Christ. As Jesus loved, so do you show the same love to your spouse...This means being faithful to God within the marriage, to God's manner, his mercy, and his new covenant -- but for the sake of your spouse. Do you see the richness of this marriage work, this task? It invites the loving God to come and dwell between you."

The strength of this work lies not only in the theological maturity and the practical advice, but in the personal stories interspersed throughout the work - the stories that touch the reader as a whole person and speak more effectively than any explanation could. And the beauty and love which have developed in the author's own marriage give the reader the hope that relationships can grow, change, and deepen in spite of our failures and blindness to the marriage partner. The reader feels privileged as he/she is allowed to share in the intimacy of another couple's marriage, to learn and grow from these honest experiences. And as Wangerin summarizes what his marriage has done for him, the beauty of a marriage relationship even with its shortcomings and self-centeredness but which includes as its center the love of God is revealed:

> "The events of our marriage haven't been lost on
> me. This is the message of my remembering - that
> none of it has gone unrecognized...No writing can

account for the mystery or the strength of these...years....The gifts that you have given me, they've taught me its name. It's name is love. You love me.

"What would we have done if you hadn't found ways to let me know? Oh, we would have survived well enough. But we wouldn't have been so rich.

"We would have made a marriage of it, I am sure. But I wouldn't have seen the living face of my Lord Jesus Christ so clearly or so closely."

Like his marriage book, his book on death is mature, practical and reinforced throughout with personal stories and memories which allow the reader to experience as well as understand the idea presented. Again his style is straight forward, honest, looking directly at the pain, suffering, and separation caused by death (in all of its forms), yet allowing the reader hope even in the midst of this stark presentation of death. As Katie Androski states: "The writing is clear, precise, and bare, which can be terrifying, like a skull, when the subject is death....But Mourning into Dancing is a Pastor's invitation to sit with him while he sketches the causes of sadness. He names them and tells a story or two along the way." And the reader can find his/her own experience therein.

Wangerin involves the reader immediately in his work, as he does in all of his writings, by beginning in the middle, then working backwards to explain the beginning statements to the reader. The first page of Mourning into Dancing begins: "Uninvited, unappreciated. Feared, in fact. Abhorred! There comes to any party, at any time, one who causes such dismay and hatred that the people respond by not responding at all: they ignore her.

"They know they can't command her...She'll do as she pleases... Though she continues to stand beside them, breathing against their necks, they dance the fervid, grinning dances, by motion alone denying her presence until she touches them, one by one or two by two, and the game is up, and the dance is done, and none can refuse her. None. And then her name is on the lips of those whose dancing she destroyed. Her name is-----"

After this ominous introduction to the work, the author begins to tell the story of his daughter's sixteenth birthday party, and he begins setting up the contrast throughout the book between his daughter (and most young people) who think they are in control and can handle anything, and the uninvited guest at the party whom no one controls and who can destroy everyone. "I tell you truly: at that moment, affected by the craft and the talent, the marvelous unity, the utter confidence, the allegiance and strength of this communion of children, I was indeed able to believe Talitha (ain't nothing I can't handle)...I almost wept with the glad perception: Yes...There is nothing, there is no one you and your friends can't handle together.

"I was, I say, inclined that way -- till that guest came whom no one controls, against whom no party nor any person is ever safe."

After telling another story of a phone call that came during his daughter's party, Wangerin again picks up his theme: "Uninvited, unappreciated, feared, and despised, the terrible guest had come to my daughter's party....

"She comes in a hundred forms, ten of which, at least, she wore that night. Abuse is one such form. Divorce is another. The division of children and parents... Sheer, fearsome anonymity is a fourth...Self-despising and despair and the cruelty of human loneliness -- these are her forms.

> "Her name is Death.
> ...No one, no one could 'handle' it.
> Not when it is Death.
> I cried for my daughter's outrageous ignorance."

"There is no party Death does not crash. There is no time she does not shadow. And the only way we blunt and cover her presence is by dancing in blind denial. She is here. Wherever there is live, Death walks the boundaries. She is here, even now. And she will work her will despite the dances, all the dances..."

After forcing the reader to face the omnipresence of death without the usual euphemisms to avoid looking at it, Wangerin then defines death, both large and small deaths which we all experience and discusses the styles of grieving and of healing which can occur if we truthfully acknowledge the many deaths in our lives and the fact of our own personal death. For the sake of the study, Wangerin defines death as the "sundering of any real relationship --- a little death or a death of traumatic consequences, but death. It's the sundering that's always the same.

> "And sadness follows.
> And the name of sadness, is grief.
> When we die, we grieve."

With this definition Wangerin is able to involve each reader in his study, for each of us has experienced the sundering of small or large relationships, and "Death doesn't wait till the ends of our lives to meet us and to make an end. Instead, we die a hundred times before we die; and all the little endings on the way are like a slowly growing echo of the final Bang! before that bang takes place."

Many pages are written by Wangerin in his attempt to get the reader to stop his/her ignoring of death and of grief because he believes that "most of us spend a good deal of energy and intellect avoiding the notion of death altogether." But he also believes that it is better to know the griefs that overtake us. "It is always better to know its name, infinitely better to understand the process that shall continue to involve us or else we will (like children) resist and fight as if against an enemy. In fact, grief is not an enemy. It hurts, to be sure. But it is the hurt of healing. Grief is the grace of God within us, the natural process of recovery for those who have suffered death."

Throughout this work Wangerin realistically shows the horrors and pain of death but always contrasts it to the healing, grace, and good news of Christ's triumph over death. And he emphasizes the victory over death in Christ, and constantly points the reader to this "present Savior with whom we meet and wrestle death." Because of this victory in Christ, we don't need to ignore the enemy, death, as the fearful world does. As a matter of fact, Wangerin shows that the more realistically we face and recognize death around us, "the sweeter will the love of our Lord be."

Wangerin's work is realistic, pragmatic and comforting even though throughout he forces the reader not only to acknowledge death and the many small deaths of life because he constantly shows that this acknowledgment of grief enables us to allow Christ's comfort in our daily lives. In fact, to Wangerin, without this acknowledgment of daily griefs and deaths, we don't appreciate the daily presence of Christ. "If the Gospel seems irrelevant to our daily lives, that is our fault, not the Gospel's. For if death is not a daily reality, then Christ's triumph over death is neither daily nor real. Worship and proclamation and even faith itself take on a dream-like, unreal air, and Jesus is reduced to something like a long-term insurance policy, filed and forgotten -- whereas he can be a necessary ally, an immediate, continuing friend, the Holy Destroyer of Death and the Devil, my own beautiful Savior."

Edna Hinz states that Wangerin does not "make light of our troubles, or promise to double our joys or cut our trouble in half, or remove our grief with proverbs and Bible verses or shame us for even having troubles. He is too honest a writer to whitewash facts. Christians die and Christians sorrow. Christians flub, fail, and lose their jobs. Christians are not spared natural disasters...Christians do indeed have griefs...But those who seek resurrection from grief will surely find the way to it in this book -- that is, they will be led to Him who is the Way."

Wangerin very effectively uses his personal, pastoral style, and, as is his vocation "he tells stories (to allow the reader to feel as well as to understand the ideas): Biblical ones like how death came into the world through Adams' sin; personal stories about his daughter Talitha and growing up, one about Terri Jackson whose house burned down; about a surgery removing part of Wangerin's lung; about his memories of his Father when he learned by letter that his Father had cancer; and about Gloria, whose beloved uncle, Sonny Boy, a dancer, died, and how she grieved. Wangerin mixes these stories with his explanations and meditations." (Katie Androski, p. 33)

And as in all his works, in spite of his blunt, realistic, unadorned looking at life and its griefs, he ends his work on hope and resurrection. "This, too, is part of grieving -- not as the end and the absence of it, but as part of its purpose and its success -- this: Rising to life again...In Christ, we have peace. Shalom: health and wholeness of life again, the promise he made the day before he went down to the Pit: Peace I leave with you; my peace I give to you; not as the world gives do I give to you. Let not your heart be troubled, neither let it be afraid. In this world you have tribulation; but be of good cheer, I have overcome this world."

Wangerin's deep belief in Christ and the resurrection doesn't allow him to deny the harshness, grief, or reality of death. As he states: "But I shall not perish....No, this is not a wishful denial of the reality nor some incompleteness of death. My body will die. Every single relationship in which I now experience life -- every relationship! -- will break. I will at once lose my place in the created world and family and friends and breathing; my reason, my senses, and all my strength, yes and my self -- until the darkness is complete, until I am, from earthly perspectives, a nothing in a nowhere. I will die.

"But I will not perish...
I carry to the grave this promise: that God so loved
the world that he gave his only Son, that whoever
believes in him should not perish...but have eternal
life."

And the purpose of grief in the face of death, according to
Wangerin? "It smacks us with the Truth -- the Truth we all deny
-- that we are finite, and we struggle to prove ourselves strong,
but grief brings us to the limits of our own strength....God does
not assault us or cause us sorrows in order to draw us back to him.
God, rather, waits -- waits upon us, waits to show mercy to
us...And we become a child. Helpless, needy, weak, returning to
God and by Jesus to the kingdom of Heaven...This is the purpose
of grieving then:

"Always to return the bereaved back to life...
And this too is the purpose of grieving: In the same
manner to turn all of those bereaved of the primal,
divine relationship back to God, to his love and to that
life that cannot be taken away from them, forever.
This is joy most serene. And lo: it cometh of sorrow."

In Wangerin's third book-length non-fictional work, Little
Lamb, Who Made Thee?, all of his themes come together as he
discusses, tells stories about and develops his Christian vision
concerning relationships -- child/parent relationships, adult/par-
ent relationships, family relationships. In his now very familiar
method Wangerin interweaves his theology and life convictions
with his story telling ability, merging learning and experiencing
together for the reader. And as the Introductory notes describe:
"This book's value is not just in its many wonderful insights into
parenthood...or its powerful portraits of adolescence...or its rollicking humor...No, this book is important because on a deep
level it isn't really about children and parents at all -- in spite of
its subtitle. It's about maturity -- spiritual maturity -- at all ages,
a process that starts in childhood and should be continuing when
we enter, as the author says, that 'city brighter than the sunlight.'
Young people and old people, as Walter Wangerin describes,
aren't all that much different from each other. We all battle sin
and lethargy and selfishness and lack of love, and as a result,
we're equally perpetual beginners in the tasks of growing, learning wisdom, finding maturity."

166

And in this work, like all of his works, Wangerin confronts the harsh realities of life and doesn't minimize the griefs and fears, but he tells these in the context of stories, our daily stories and the eternal story, and by so doing, enables us to face the harsh chaos of life and to see the cosmos of God behind it. He, like Madelaine L'Engle "doesn't get much comfort from facts. We all believe in facts. We certainly don't need faith, not for facts. Faith is for the part of our stories that superficially aren't believable. Miracles? Resurrections? Unrealistic. Childish. Or is it not so much childish as child hearted?...In this world...it is not easy or painless or reasonable to be a Christian -- that is to be one who actually dares to believe that the power that created all of the galaxies, all the stars in their courses, limited that power to the powerlessness of an ordinary human baby. And what a story it is! It begins with conception, with creation, and moves on through life and death to resurrection...and most of it is impossible in ordinary terms of provable fact." (Madelaine L'Engle, p. 21)

And Wangerin does not try to be an apologist for the faith or to "prove" it, but he does tell the story of God throughout all of his works so that we can see how our small stories are part of the Divine story. "Truth may be proffered like pennies in doctrines. But Holy Truth, the core force, is a living thing and desires relationship with the people, who seek relationship with it. Story is the meeting place in which relationships begin, mature, may be experienced whole, may be named, are certainly remembered, live....And story is not story till it's told. And the telling is the one critical duty of a religious leader after all." ("Telling Tales,"p. 39)

And since Wangerin wants to relieve the confusions of his readers not teach intellectually but comfort them wholistically, he tells stories throughout Little Lamb, Who Made Thee?. Once again Wangerin forces the reader to realistically look at life, and especially the brutal life that will soon assault the children of the world and our own children and ourselves.

> "The children haven't long before the world assaults them...Soon enough they'll meet faces immeasurably enraged. Soon enough they'll be accused of things they did not do. Soon enough they will suffer guilt at the hands of powerful people who can't accept their own guilt and who must dump it, therefore, on the weak.... Sorrows shall surely come -- but surely parents, not through us!"

167

After his opening introduction urging us to create golden moments and laughter for these children to whom sorrows will surely come, he then begins telling stories of his childhood, looking for God, his growing awareness of fear and danger, and his experiencing of grace. Then as the reader through the stories truly feels these concepts of divine/human interaction in our daily lives, Wangerin urges his reader to become like children, and his chapter Eight begins:

"Give us, O Lord, clear eyes, uncomplicated hearts, and guileless tongues. Make us like children again!"

And childhood encompasses many aspects that as we are going through it toward teenagehood we desire to lose, but as we become adults we realize we need to regain:

"When we are children we're likelier to be kinder because we are small in an overwhelming world, and smallness keeps us humble.

When we are children we are likelier to be more honest...

When we are wide-eyed children the world is filled with things both visible and invisible...

When we were children we laughed without embarrassment.

When we were children we would gasp with delight at a sudden, beautiful thing, yearning to touch it. We didn't worry whether our notion of beauty was naive.

When we were children our loving was given immediate expression. We said it. We showed it.

When we were children we accepted forgiveness completely.

Oh sisters and brothers...it is as little children that we shall enter the kingdom of heaven."

As he tells stories of teenagehood, our departures from childhood, the dangers and joys of growing up and being children, adolescents, teens and parents, he brings in stories about Dorothy, his sister-in-law who has Down's Syndrome. Dorothy, whom the world considers retarded but through whose eyes Wangerin sees and enables us to see childlikeness. "Retarded? Who is the fool who says so? This woman has an apprehension of the universe more intimate and more devout than my own. Her knowing is not troubled by extraneous thought...I had been to Holden Village three times before that Summer (when Dorothy went with them), but I had never seen with primal eyes until I stood with Dorothy looking up and sighing....She was the quick one. My responses were baffled and slow. She was the one who trained me both in seeing and in speaking. I...in simple creation -- was the retarded one. How often we get it backward. How much we miss when we do!" And later he states: "And in another sense you (Dorothy) are more mature than most of my acquaintances....And I said in my soul, no, but Dorothy is different from us after all. She is better. She loves more quickly and with less confusion.

"Ah, Dorothy. I think God honors hearts more than brains. You are the image of God in my world. In you the best of the child continues, while the best of adulthood emerges."

And Wangerin unifies this work on children, adolescents, teenagers, parents and old age, by the internal theme coming through all the stories and theology: "Unless you turn and become like little children, you will never enter into the kingdom of heaven." And he urges each of us to become childlike, full of wonder, "sensitive to spiritual things, quick to sense the motions of God's Spirit, alive to the love of God that surrounds us and open to his forgiveness." And we are further encouraged to be open to this God and to live for him. If this growth in trust and childlikeness occurs, then when we become dependent and child-like once again in old age, we are ready to be welcomed into God's home as his children. "And God will wipe away all tears from our eyes." This humble childlike faith in the Father's love enables us when once again we fear the darkness as we did as children, to trust that God will be there to comfort us even as the darkness surrounds us in death."

Wangerin departs from his normal style when he writes Reliving the Passion, a meditation for the Forty Days of Lent. Although his story telling animates the experiences of Christ's passions, the writing has less objective distance, and the writer, narrator, reader are more intimately connected. And the use of the first person plural throughout brings the reader and author together in a unity of struggle, confession and belief. We and Wangerin are there as the events in Mark are retold and meditated upon. And the questions raised by the author are our questions, and we as readers must answer them, and just as Wangerin's Pastor

Father translated Wangerin as a young boy to the time of Christ and enabled him to experience the events as present, so we the reader are transported so we can hear and experience the sacred story. Wangerin's intent in the book is to "lead the reader step by step to an Easter celebration, walking with Jesus both in thought (learning along the way) and in a genuine feeling (experiencing the Way -- experiencing the love of the Lord in his passion.) The time distinction between the time of Christ and our present time is erased by Wangerin so that we are there and the events are occurring in our time. Just as on the Mt. of Transfiguration, time is collapsed as Moses, Elijah, and Christ all speak together, so Wangerin collapses time in the meditation and brings the reader into kairos (God's time) where past, present and future all merge together and chronological time becomes meaningless or at least irrelevant as the reader contemplates the events of Lent.

The Introduction to this work summarizes well what Wangerin desires to happen in each of his works: "Earnestly I pray blessings upon the hours we are about to spend together -- that your hearts may grow young again and that like children in sorrow, like children in joy, you finally cry in the silence of souls, I love you, Lord Jesus. I do!"

PRIMARY BIBLIOGRAPHY - BOOKS

Wangerin, Walter Jr.

. . . .As for me and my House. Nashville: Thomas Nelson, 1987.

. . . The Bible, its Story for Children. MacMillan/Checkerboard, 1981.

. . .The Book of God. Grand Rapids: Zondervan, 1996.

. . .The Book of Sorrows. San Francisco: Harper & Row, 1985.

. . .The Book of the Dunn Cow. Chicago: Rand McNally, 1978.

. . .Branta and the Golden Stone. New York: Simon & Schuster Books for
      Young Readers, 1993.

. . .The Crying for a Vision. New York: Simon & Schuster Books for Young
      Readers, 1994.

. . .Elizabeth and the Water Troll. New York: Harper Collins, 1991.

. . .In the Beginning there was No Sky. Nashville: Thomas Nelson, 1986.

. . .Little Lamb, Who Made Thee? Grand Rapids: Zondervan, 1993.

. . .The Manger is Empty. San Francisco: Harper & Row, 1989.

. . .A Miniature Cathedral and Other Poems. San Francisco: Harper & Row, 1987.

. . .Miz Lil and the Chronicles of Grace. San Francisco: Harper & Row, 1988.

. . .Mourning into Dancing. Grand Rapids: Zondervan, 1992.

. . .My First Book about Jesus. Chicago: Rand McNally, 1983.

. . .Orphean Passages. San Francisco: Harper & Row, 1986.

. . .Potter. Elgin: Chariot, 1985.

. . .Ragman and Other Cries of Faith. San Francisco: Harper & Row, 1984.

. . .Reliving the Passion. Grand Rapids: Zondervan, 1992.

. . .Thistle. New York: Harper & Row, 1983.

. . .Una Sancta

Wangerin, Walter Jr., Gail McGrew Eifrig, ed.

. . .Measuring the Days. San Francisco: Harper, 1993.

PRIMARY BIBLIOGRAPHY - ARTICLES

Wangerin, Walter Jr. "The Altar of Motherhood." The Lutheran May 1990: 5.

. . ."Anonymity and Anger." The Lutheran Mar. 1993: 5.

. . ."Are you the Fool I take you for?" The Lutheran Oct. 1991: 5.

. . ."Arthur Forte, Foul and Old." Lutheran Vision Jan. 1995: 7.

. . ."Artists Enshrine a Neighborhood, and Those Living There." Evansville Courier 23 June 1984: 3-4.

. . ."As for me and my House." Christian Reader Sept. 1987: 98-113.

. . ."Ashamed of Jesus." The Lutheran June 1995: 5.

. . ."Ashes, Ashes, All Fall Down." The Lutheran Mar. 1994: 5.

. . ."Assessment." The Lutheran Sept. 1993: 5.

. . ."Baby Hannah of the Womb of God." Lutheran Partners Nov. 1987: 8-11.

. . ."Between Noon and Three." LCA Partners Apr. 1982: 24-29.

. . ."The Bike Report." The Lutheran Sept. 1988: 5.

. . ."A Bird for the Incarnation." The Lutheran Dec. 1988: 5.

. . ."Bless my Beloved when I Cannot." Hospice Newsletter Sept. 1994.

. . ."A Bright Annunciation of Angels." Cresset Dec. 1992: 11-14.

. . ."But if I am not a Sheep." Interaction June 1975: 27-30.

. . ."But what Do Thanks Do?" Lutheran Vision Nov. 1994: 7.

. . ."Butter! Butter! Butter!" The Other Side Apr. 1988: 34-35.

. . ."Calitha Wangia, Go! Go! Go!" The Lutheran Aug. 1992: 5.

. . ."Can a Judgment Day be Good?" Lutheran Vision Nov. 1994: 7.

. . ."The Canticle of the Sun." The Lutheran May 1994: 5.

. . ."The Centurion." Moody Monthly Apr. 1992: 55-56.

. . ."The Chair in the First Row." The Lutheran Nov. 1990: 5.

. . ."The Cherry Tree." Pursuit 3.3 (undated): 20-21.

. . ."Child, be Born in us Today!" Lutheran Vision Dec. 1994: 7.

. . ."Children have Role in Death's Drama." Evansville Courier Nov. 1985.

. . ."The Christ Mass..." Currents in Theology and Mission Dec. 1986: 326-334.

. . ."Christ our Forgiveness Right Now." Lutheran Vision Mar. 1995: 7.

. . ."Christian Writer in Today's World Faces 'Double Trouble.'" Evansville Courier 18 Oct. 1986: 5-6.

. . ."A Christmas Pastorale." Christianity Today Dec. 1982: 26-28.

. . ."The Christmas Story—Retold." Lutheran Vision Dec. 1994: 7.

. . ."Clara Schreiber, Writer." Lutheran Vision Jan. 1995: 7.

. . ."Commencement." The Lutheran July 1989: 5.

. . ."Concerning Communion." The Lutheran May 1992: 5.

. . ."Confirming our Faith Outloud." Lutheran Vision Oct. 1994: 7.

. . ."County Fair." The Lutheran Aug. 1990: 5.

. . ."The Crying for a Vision." The Lutheran Oct. 1994: 5.

. . ."Dancing in the Dark." The Lutheran Feb. 1988: 5.

. . ."Daughtertalk." The Lutheran Mar. 1991: 5.

. . ."The Democratic Ethic." The Lutheran Nov. 1989: 5.

. . ."Divine Difference." Readers' Digest Dec. 1989: 110.

. . ."Dr. Martin Luther King - The Measure of this Great Man." Evansville Courier 11 Jan. 1986: 3-4.

. . ."Don't Hide behind Enemy Lines." Salt Mar. 1992: 29-30.

. . ."Dorothy—in the Crown of God." The Lutheran Sept. 1989: 5.

. . ."Dorothy, my Sister-in-Love." Christianity Today Aug. 1984: 66.

. . ."Easter: And all Nature sings." The Lutheran Apr. 1, 1988: 5.

. . ."Educating the Human Spirit." The Lutheran Mar. 1988: 5.

. . . ."The Education of Matthew Wangerin." Christianity Today May 1991: 14-19.

PRIMARY BIBLIOGRAPHY- ARTICLES

. . ."An Effusion on 2 Corinthians 5:21." The Lutheran Apr. 1993: 5.

. . . Evansville Courier, Evansville, IN. weekly columns - Apr. 4, 1981 - Mar. 8, 1988.

. . .Evansville Press, Evansville, IN. weekly columns from Apr. 1988 - Jan. 1993.

. . ."An Excerpt: Ashes, Ashes." Christianity Today Feb. 1987: 53.

. . ."The Exploding Body." The Lutheran Apr. 1989: 5.

. . ."The Eye of the Farmer." The Lutheran Sept. 1988: 5.

. . ."Faithful Thought: Demeaned and Forgettable?" Christianity Today Nov. 1983: 56.

. . ."Family Gatherings." Christian Reader Jan. 1994: 93-102.

. . ."Fifty." The Lutheran July 1994: 5.

. . ."The Fish the Disciples Caught." The Lutheran June 1993: 5.

. . ."Fishing, my Friend and I." The Lutheran Feb. 1991: 5.

. . ."Five Figures of Jesus." The Lutheran Mar. 1995: 5.

. . ."Flying the Night Wind." Christianity Today Apr. 1990: 23-26.

. . ."The Fourth Cross." Servant Mar. 1994: 3-5.

. . ."Gas Pump Parable." Christian Reader Jan. 1987: 38-40.

. . ."Gentle into that Good Night." Christian Home and School May 1990: 16-19.

. . ."Gift of a Job can Help Youths Break out of the Circle of Welfare."
        Evansville Courier 8 Feb. 1986: 4-5.

. . ."God Save Africa." The Lutheran Apr. 1988: 5.

. . ."God Speed Thee on thy Journey." The Lutheran Nov. 1990: 5.

. . ."Going Home." The Lutheran Feb. 1994: 5.

. . ."Gonna Sing, my Lord, for all that I'm Worth." The Presbyterian Record
. . .Sept. 1988: 18-23.

. . ."Grace Encountered." The Lutheran June 1988: 5.

. . ."Grace in Marriage." Christian Home and School Mar. 1988: 34.

. . ."And Grace my Fears Relieved." Discipleship Journal Jan. 1994: 56-57.

. . ."Grace Taught my Heart to Fear." Presbyterian Record Sept. 1994: 22-23.

. . . ."Grandpa Wangerin, Shepherd and Guardian." Lutheran Vision Feb. 1995: 7.

. . ."The Great Reversal." Christianity Today Mar. 1989: 19+.

. . ."The Habit of Goodness." The Lutheran Oct. 1990: 5.

. . ."Hallowed be Thy Name." The Lutheran Oct. 1992: 5.

. . ."Have you Got a Minute? Will you Give it to the Shy?" Evansville
        Courier 3 Oct. 1987: 6-7.

. . ."He Suffered the Consequence of our Sin." Lutheran Vision Mar. 1995: 7.

. . ."He who has Cried, 'I Can't!'" The Lutheran July 1993: 5.

. . ."The Hidden Promise." Lutheran Vision Nov. 1994: 7.

. . ."Holiness is a Way of Life - not Just an Hour Each Week." Evansville
        Courier 16 Nov. 1985: 7-8.

. . ."Holy People." Lutheran Standard Mar. 1983.

. . ."The House where Mrs. Story Used to Live." Wittenburg Door June 1986: 25+.

. . ."How to Say NO to Adultery." Our Family June 1990: 4-8.

. . ."A Hug as Holy as the Ocean." The Lutheran May 1988: 5.

. . ."I Love Thee, Baby B." The Lutheran Jan. 1989: 5.

. . ."In Baptism we Begin." Lutheran Vision Oct. 1994: 7.

. . ."In Praise of Lady Liberty - America, the Good Land." Evansville
        Courier 21 June 1986: 3-4.

. . ."In Praise of Lady Liberty - the Diversity of her People." Evansville
        Courier 28 June 1986: 5-6.

. . ."Jerome Got Up to Sing." The Lutheran Sept. 1994: 5.

. . ."Joseph's Complaint." Currents Feb. 1994: 52.

. . ."The Joys of Parenting." Parents and Teenagers June 1990: 7.

. . ."Judas and Me." Christianity Today Apr. 1992: 18-19.

. . ."Just Say Whoa!" The Lutheran May 1991: 5.

. . ."Keepsake." Reformed Journal May 1988: 19.

. . ."Killing with a Word." The Lutheran June 1992: 5.

. . ."Lady Liberty, your Freedoms make you Beautiful!" Evansville Courier
      19 July 1986: 3-4.

. . ."Leaving for Cleaving." The Lutheran May 1993: 5.

. . ."Lessons from the Book of Matthew." Salt Feb. 1994: 17-22.

. . ."Letting Go." Christianity Today Sept. 1986: 26-27.

. . ."Life in Frontlines Ministry." Lifelines 6.1, Apr. 1990: 2-8.

. . ."Lily." The Lutheran Apr. 1992: 5.

. . ."Listen to your History." The Lutheran Jan. 1988: 5.

. . ."Little Children, can you Tell...?" The Lutheran Dec. 1989: 5.

. . ."Little Lamb Who Made Thee?" Christian Reader Jan. 1994: 5.

. . ."Live Long on the Earth." The Lutheran Jan. 1990: 5.

. . ."The Lord's Prayer, Agonized." The Lutheran Mar. 1990: 5.

. . ."Lost in he Story." The Lutheran Mar. 1989: 5.

. . ."Love is Patient and Kind." The Lutheran Aug. 1989: 5.

. . ."The Making of a Minister." Christianity Today Sept. 1982: 16-18.

. . ."Mama, Mama, who are you?" The Lutheran June 1994: 5.

. . ."The Manger is Empty." Christianity Today Dec. 1985: 20-25.

. . ."Martin Luther, a Bold Obedience." Lutheran Vision Feb. 1995: 7.

. . ."Martin Luther King, Jr., Preacher." Lutheran Vision Jan. 1995: 7.

. . ."A Matter of Being, and a Matter of Being Right." Christian Century
      July 1987: 591-594.

. . ."Matthew 7, 8 and 9." Moody Monthly Jan. 1990: 22-29.

. . ."Meeting Jesus." Lutheran Vision Oct. 1994: 7.

. . ."Miss Augustine, Second Grade Teacher." Lutheran Vision Feb. 1995: 7.

. . ."Mizpah: The Watch Post between us." The Lutheran Aug. 1994: 5.

. . ."Mosquito." Christian Century Jan. 1979: 21.

. . ."A Moving Flint." Image Sept. 1994: 7-12.

. . ."My Father's Christmas Surprise." Lutheran Dec. 1985: 5-7.

. . ."My Genuine Reformation." Lutheran Vision Oct. 1994: 7.

. . ."My Hoary Head is Happy." The Lutheran Jan. 1989: 5.

. . ."My own Magnificat." The Lutheran Dec. 1991: 5.

. . ."Night of the Shattering Glass." The Lutheran Nov. 1993: 5.

. . ."No Fields of Yellow Flowers Anymore." Insight 1992: 20-24.

. . ."No More Crying There." Moody Monthly June 1987: 55-57.

. . ."No Sky." Cumberland Presbyterian Nov. 1993: 20-21.

. . ."Not by my own Reason or Strength." The Lutheran Nov. 1988: 5.

. . ."O Brave New World, that has No People in it!" NY Times. Book
      Review Mar. 1993.

. . ."Of Cowlicks and Confirmation." The Lutheran May 1989: 5.

. . ."Of Mountains and Making Decisions." Lutheran Vision Oct. 1994: 7.

. . ."Of Seeds and Love and Legacies." The Lutheran May 1995: 5.

. . ."Oh, my Dear, the Dying!" The Lutheran Feb. 1990: 5.

. . ."Oh, what a Spectacular Sunday!" The Lutheran Apr. 1990: 5.

. . ."On Mourning the Death of a Marriage." Christianity Today May 1984: 20-23.

. . ."One Night in Bethlehem." Hodder, Church of England Newspaper 18 Dec. 1992.

. . ."Out of the Depths." The Lutheran Sept. 1992: 5.

. . ."The Pacing Preacher." The Lutheran June 1988: 5.

. . ."Painting Christmas." Christianity Today Dec. 1993: 28-30.
. . ."Parents, Unite!" The Lutheran July 1991: 5.
. . ."Passing the Torch." The Lutheran Aug. 1989: 5.
. . ."A Personal Thanksgiving." The Lutheran Nov. 1989: 5.
. . ."Picky, Picky? Yes, Indeed." Calvinist Contact May 1991: 13.
. . ."Pieta." The Lutheran Oct. 1993: 5.
. . . ."Plenitudo Temporis." Currents in Theology and Mission Dec. 1987: 419-422.
. . ."A Pocketful of Stones." The Lutheran Jan. 1988: 5.
. . ."Polycarp, Martyr." Lutheran Vision Feb. 1995: 7.
. . ."Power in Powerlessness." Christian Century Mar. 1993: 284-285.
. . ."Prayer is often Incomplete because we Forget to Listen." Evansville
        Courier 22 Oct. 1983: 5-6.
. . ."A Preacher's Story." Pulpit Digest May 1987: 26-31.
. . ."The Preposterous Thanksgiving." The Lutheran Nov. 1988: 5.
. . ."The Proud Prays Thus." The Lutheran June 1989: 5.
. . ."A Quiet Chamber Kept for Thee." Lutheran Vision Dec. 1994: 7.
. . ."The Ragman." Lutheran Vision Mar. 1995: 7.
. . ."The Ragman, the Ragman, the Christ!" Christianity Today Apr. 1982: 22-23.
. . ."Red, Red, the Blood-Red Kiss." The Lutheran Nov. 1991: 5.
        "Remembering St. Francis of Assisi and Apples and Anger."
        Evansville Courier 4 Oct. 1986: 5-6.
. . ."The 'Retarded'—The Image of God!" The Lutheran July 1992: 5.
. . ."A Review of Today's Good Writing and Good Writers." Evansville
        Courier 12 Dec. 1987: 4-5.
. . ."Rise, Dorothy, Rise." The Lutheran May 1990: 5.
. . ."The Robber and the Attic." Grapevine June 1989: 35-38.
. . ."Robert." Moody Monthly Jan. 1989: 23-26.
. . ."The Sacred Pain of Loving." Lutheran Vision Nov. 1994: 7.
. . ."Safe from the Serpent." The Lutheran Oct. 1991: 5.
. . ."St. Grampa, the Dragon Slayer." The Lutheran Dec. 1992: 5.
. . ."St. Madeleine of Crosswicks." The Lutheran Feb. 1990: 5.
. . ."Seastone." Cresset June 1994: 23.
. . ."She Cried in Secret." Worldwide Challenge Jan. 1989: 26-29.
. . ."The Slaughter of the Innocents." Trucks Nov. 1990: 10.
. . ."Small Walt." The Lutheran Feb. 1993: 5.
. . ."Snowbound." The Lutheran Jan. 1994: 5.
. . ."Some Reflections on America's Aerial Bombing of Libya." Evansville
        Courier 19 Apr. 1986: 4-5.
. . ."A Special Letter." VU Guild Bulletin Sept. 1993: 25.
. . ."Spring Cleaning." The Lutheran Apr. 1994: 5.
. . ."Stir up Thy Power—and Come!" Lutheran Vision Dec. 1994: 7.
. . ."A Story of Lenten Extremities." The Lutheran Mar. 1988: 5.
. . ."Surviving by Song." The Lutheran Mar. 1992: 5.
. . ."Taking Back the Night Together." The Lutheran Feb. 1995: 5.
. . ."Talking in Circles with God." Lutheran Standard Sept. 1986: 19.
. . ."Tell me the Joy." The Lutheran Apr. 1991: 5.
. . ."Telling Tales." Publishers Weekly 7 Mar. 1986: 39-40.
. . ."Teresa of Avila, Love and Prayer." Lutheran Vision Jan. 1995: 7.
. . ."Thaane, my Superior." Fields of Light Journal Sept. 1993: 12-13.
. . ."Them Also which Sleep in Jesus." The Lutheran Oct. 1989: 5.
. . ."Thou Shalt Not Steal." The Lutheran Nov. 1994: 5.

. . ."Things have Changed since Sinai." The Lutheran May 1989: 5.

. . ."Three Poets." The Lutheran July 1988: 5.

. . ."Throw the What Out, Bobus?" The Lutheran Feb. 1992: 5.

. . ."Time and Space and God and me." Lutheran Vision Jan. 1995: 7.

. . ."The Time in the City." Together July 1981: 3-6.

. . ."To Keep it Holy." The Lutheran Dec. 1993: 5.

. . ."To My New President." The Lutheran Jan. 1993: 5.

. . ."To the Waker, the one Alone." The Lutheran Aug. 1988: 5.

. . ."Two Pictures of Christmas." The Lutheran Dec. 1990: 5.

. . ."Unearned Suffering is Redemptive." The Lutheran Feb. 1989: 5.

. . . Untitled. Leadership Sept. 1990: 146.

. . ."Walk on Radiance, Amazed." The Lutheran June 1991: 5.

. . ."Walk with the Women." The Lutheran Apr. 1995: 5.

. . ."What is Hell?" The Lutheran Sept. 1990: 5.

. . ."What Shall we Say of King Saul's Chromosomes? Nothing!"
    Evansville Courier 7 Mar. 1987: 4-5.

. . ."What's a Good Story." Christian Reader Mar. 1991: 66-67.

. . ."When you get there, Wait!" Coming of Age Gracefully, AAL (1995).

. . ."While God Waits us Out." NY times, Book Review Oct. 1988: 40.

. . ."Who is this Person?" Evangelical Lutheran Church Marriage Partnership
    June 1991: 76-77.

. . ."Who Pastors the Pastors?" The Lutheran Mar. 1989: 5.

. . ."The Wild Geese Flying." The Lutheran Dec. 1994: 5.

. . ."Who are you, ELCA?" The Lutheran Sept. 1991: 5.

. . ."The Widow's Stone." The Lutheran Oct. 1988: 5.

. . ."Would you Look at that, Now!" Interaction Oct. 1974: 21-22.

. . ."The Writing of Branta and Other Affections." Cresset Dec. 1993: 5-8.

. . ."You are the Poet, I am the Poem." ELCA Yearbook. Colorado Springs:
    Navigators, 1994. back cover.

. . ."You are, you are, you are." The Lutheran Jan. 1990: 5.

. . ."Your Physical Examination." The Lutheran Jan. 1995: 5.

. . ."Zipping Open the Red Sea." NY Times, Book Review Nov. 1989: 48.

SECONDARY BIBLIOGRAPHY

Andraski, Katie. "The Many Deaths of Walt Wangerin." Christianity Today 8 Mar. 1993.

. . ."The Unruly Talent of Walter Wangerin." Christianity Today 17 Feb..1989: 33.

Bauman, Richard. Story, Performance, and Event. Cambridge: Cambridge UP, 1986.

Baumgaertner, Jill P. "Review of Miz Lil." Christian Century 27 Sept. 1989.

Bausch, William J. Storytelling, Imagination and Faith. Mystic: Twenty-Third, 1989.

Bettelheim, Bruno. The Use of Enchantment. Vintage Books/Random House, 1989.

Bishman, Andrea. "Wangerin Publishes New Book." The Torch 7 Oct. 1994: 6.

Bittner, Robert. "The Colors of the Calendar." Christianity Today 9 Apr. 1990: 35.

Brockelman, Paul. The Inside Story (Stories and Myth).

Church, F. Forrester. "Review of the Orphean Passages." Christian Century 19 Nov. 1986: 1044.

Clair, Maxine. "Word Up: Oral Tradition in the Pedagory of Creative Writing." Women's Studies Quarterly 3 & 4 (1993).

Cox, Harvey. The Seduction of the Spirit.

Delloff, Linda-Marie. "Year's Best Books by Lutheran." The Lutheran Jan. 1992: 61.

Dillard, Annie. Holy the Firm. New York: Harper & Row.

. . .Living by Fiction. New York: Harper & Row, 1983.

Eifrig, Gail McGrew. "Review of Elizabeth and the Water Troll." Cresset Dec. 1991: 35.

. . ."Review of Miz Lil." Currents in Theology and Mission 1989: 121-125.

Eifrig, Kate. "Review of Book of the Dunn Cow." Cresset Dec. 1991: 15.

Ellul, Jacques. The Humiliation of the Word. Trans. Joyce Main Hanks. Grand Rapids: Eerdmans, 1985.

Estes, Clarissa Pinkola. The Gift of Story. 1995.

Freitag, Michael. "The Typewriter vs. the Pulpit." The New York Times Book Review 8 Jan. 1989: 10.

Frye, Northrop. The Double Vision: Language and Meaning in Literature. University of Toronto, 1991.

. . .The Great Code. New York: Harcourt, Brace Jonanovich, 1983.

Griffin, William. "Walter Wangerin, Junior." Publishers Weekly 6 Mar. 1987.

Harding, Sarah. "Oral Narrative and the Short Story." 1993.

Heeg, Shirley. "Getting out of Life Alive." Perspectives Magazine Apr. 1993: 21-22.

Holler, Clyde. "Lakota Religion and Tragedy: The Theology of Black Elk Speaks." Journal of the American Academy of Religion 52.1 (1984).

Hong, Edna H. "Review of Mourning into Dancing." Christian Century 12 May 1993: 13.

Jahner, Elaine A., ed. Lakota Myth. University of Nebraska, 1983.

Johnson, Doug. "Growth and Failure." The Next Generation Winter 1993: 15.

Jung, Carl. Man and his Symbols. New Jersey: Doubleday, 1964.

Kelsey, Morton T. Myth, History and Faith. New York: Paulist, 1974.

Kiely, Robert. "A Fable for our Time." New York Times Book Review Winter 1978: 67, 89.

Kung, Hans. Literature and Religion. New York: Paragon, 1991.

LaGrand, Paul. "Wangerin Weaves Wonderful Woe." The Chimes 21 Oct. 1994.

L'Engle, Madeleine. The Rock that is Higher: Story as Truth. Wheaton: Harold
     Shaw, 1993.
. . .Walking on Water: Reflections on Faith and Art. New York: Bantam, 1980.
Malone, Michael. "The Cosmos and the Farmyard." The New York Times
     11 Aug. 1985: Sec. 7.
Marty, Martin E. "Review of As for me and my House." The Lutheran 1 May 1987.
Maxwell, H. Story as a Way to God. Resources Publications.
May, Rollo. The Cry for Myth. New York: W. W. Norton, 1991.
. . .Symbolism in Religion and Literature. New York: Braziller, 1960.
Miller, Calvin. Spirit, Word and Story. Word, 1989.
Miller, Roger. "Religion and Faith." Milwaukee Journal 25 Dec. 1988.
. . .Words with Power. New York: Harcourt, Brace Jovanovich, 1990.
. . .Spiritus Mundi. Essays on Literature. Myth and Society. Bloomington:
     Indiana UP, 1976.
Oberdeck, John W. "Review of Mourning into Dancing." Concordia Journal
     Jan. 1993: 84-85.
Owens, Virginia Stem. "Walter Wangerin and the Cosmic Equation."
Christian Century Dec. 1994: 1190-1192.
. . ."Walter Wangerin's Branta." Cresset Dec. 1993: 26-28.
Patrick, Jean. "Storyteller Sees Christmas Anew." The Daily Republic 1 Dec. 1989.
Payne, Peggy. "God's Inner-City Go-Between." The New York Times Book
     Review 8 Jan. 1989: 9-10.
Peterson, Eugene H. "Charting the Territory of Evil." Christianity Today
     15 Oct. 1985: 50-53.
Powers, William. "Cosmology and the Reinvention of Culture: The Lakota Case."
Canadian Journal of Native Studies 7.2 (1987).
Publishers Weekly. "Review of In the Beginning there was no Sky." 28 Nov. 1986.
Reber, Jack. "Sorrow Ends Story of Dunn Cow." San Diego Tribune 21 June 1985.
Rice, Julian. "How Lakota Stories Keep the Spirit and Feed the Ghost."
     American Indian Quarterly 8.4 (1984).
. . .Lakota Storytelling. New York: Peter Lans, 1990.
. . ."An Ohunkakan Brings a Virgin Back to Camp." American Indian
     Quarterly 7.4 (1983).
. . ."Symbols: Meat for the Soul in Cheyenne Myth and Lakota Ritual."
     Western American Literature 18.2 (1983).
Richter, William. Myth and Literature. Routledge and Kegan Paul, 1975.
Rossow, Francis C. "Review of the Orphean Passages." Concordia Journal
     Oct. 1987: 395-398.
Rubel, Warren. "Winding Downward." Currents in Theology and Mission
     Aug. 1986: 197-204.
Sauer, James L. "Listen: Chaunteclear is Crowing." Eternity Dec. 1985.
Simpkinson, Charles, Anne Simpkinson, eds. Sacred Stories: A Celebration of
     the Power of Stories to Transform and Heal. San Francisco: Harper, 1993.
Spencer, William David. "Review of As for me and my House." Eternity
     Sept. 1987.

Steinke, Peter L. "Review of Ragman and Other Cries of Faith." Christian
    Century 6 Feb. 1987: 158.
Stillman, Paul. Introduction to Myth. Hayden, 1977.
Timmerman, John H. "Review of Mourning into Dancing." Christian Schools
    International 6 May 1993: 13.
    . . ."Wince with Wonder." Christianity Today 12 Dec. 1986: 60-61.
Vickery, John. Myth and Literature. University of Nebraska, 1966.
Wagoner, Walter D. "Review of the Book of Sorrows." Eternity 17 July 1985: 24.
Welty, Eudora. The Eye of the Story. New York: Vintage International, 1983.
White, Edward M. "Dunn Cow: Barnyard of Delights." Los Angeles Times
    28 Dec. 1978: 4.
Wilson, John. "The Greatest Story Ever Retold." Christianity Today 8 April 1996.
Wojahn, Karen Ann. "Celebrating the Seasons of Life." The Episcopal News
    Mar. 1990.
Yancey, Philip, ed. Reality and the Vision. Dallas: Word, 1990.
Zibart, Eve. "Good Battles Evil." Washington Post Book World (undated).